The Truth Seeker

Augustine

The Truth Seeker

Augustine

K. C. Murdarasi

CF4·K

For Susannah

10 9 8 7 6 5 4 3 2 1
© Copyright 2014 K. C. Murdarasi
paperback ISBN 978-1-78191-296-6
epub ISBN 978-1-78191-362-8
mobi ISBN 978-1-78191-363-5

Published by
Christian Focus Publications,
Geanies House, Fearn, Tain, Ross-shire,
IV20 1TW, Scotland, U.K.
Tel: +44 (0)1862 871011
Fax: +44 (0)1862 871699
www.christianfocus.com
email: info@christianfocus.com

Cover design by Daniel van Straaten
Cover illustration by Jeff Anderson
American English is used throughout this book
Printed and bound in Denmark by Nørhaven

Thanks go to Professor Greg Woolf, for help and guidance with
the research, and to Christina Rutherdale and Ann Manwell for
help with the *Thinking Further Topics*. Thanks also go, of course, to
the One who helps us when we try, and hears us when we pray.

Contents

A Brush with Death

Augustine swirled water around his clay cup, listening to the gentle sloshing noise. He swirled it harder, making some of the glistening water splash over the side of the cup and fall onto his bare knees and dusty feet. *Is this what the sea is like?* he wondered, closing his eyes as he tried to imagine a cup of water big enough to separate Africa, where he lived, from Italy, the center of the Roman Empire. It must be scary to cross it! Augustine had never seen the sea, but he was curious about it. The countryside around his villa was covered with olive groves and fir trees and fields of wheat as far as the eye could see. He knew that somewhere, far away to the north, lay the Mediterranean Sea – "Our Sea" as Romans called it because the Roman Empire stretched the whole way around the edge. Augustine had never been further than Thagaste, the town where he lived.

It wasn't just the sea Augustine was curious about. He was interested in plants and birds and animals. In his spare time he liked to wander the countryside with his friends, chasing lizards and birds, and sometimes watching the birds catch the lizards. He had just begun flicking at the water with his fingers, imagining tiny ships tossed about in his stormy cup, when a slave came into the courtyard to call him.

"Master Augustine, it's time to go to school."

"No-o!" groaned Augustine. For a wild moment he thought about running away and hiding in the olive groves until school had finished, but he knew it was no use. His father, Patrick, would find out and beat him, and then he would get sent back to school and the teacher would beat him. Plus, his mother, Monica, would give him one of her disappointed looks, and that was almost worse than a beating. Augustine loved his mother, and he wanted to make her proud of him, but even for her he couldn't pretend to enjoy school. The slave said again, "Master Augustine!"

Sighing, Augustine got up to follow her, pouring his little sea onto the dusty soil of the courtyard as he went.

Monica was a Christian, and even though her husband Patrick was a pagan, he had allowed his wife to bring up Augustine and his brother and sisters as Christians. Augustine said his prayers as his mother had taught him, and every time he prayed he asked God not to let him be beaten at school any more, but it never seemed to work. He would forget his lesson or spell something wrongly, and the teacher would cane him. It happened most of all in Greek classes. Augustine hated Greek! It was bad enough having to learn how to read and write in Latin, his own language, but reading and writing in Greek was impossible! Augustine would have been happy to make sacrifices to his father's gods, too, if he thought it would help—to mighty Saturn and the Heavenly Goddess—but he knew that they were just stories, not real gods. Even Patrick, who was supposed to believe in them, wasn't especially careful about remembering to sacrifice to them.

Augustine tried to look casual as he walked from his family villa into the town of Thagaste. The school was in an old building near the small forum, or central square. The classroom walls were covered in crumbling plaster and scribbles on the walls from generations of boys. The teacher was already talking so Augustine slipped in quietly and sat down next to one of his friends. That was one good thing about school—he had made a lot of friends.

"What is the lesson about?" he asked in a whisper.

"Dido and Aeneas, from Virgil's *Aeneid*," replied the other boy. Augustine smiled. This was the only bit of his lessons that he actually liked, the stories from ancient legends. Already he knew bits of the poem the *Aeneid* by heart and would recite the poetry to himself to enjoy its rhythm. The story of Dido was so sad that it made him want to cry, but it was a nice feeling too. The teacher was telling them about each word in the passage, explaining what type of word it was and why Virgil had chosen it, but Augustine was hardly listening to that. He was thinking about poor Dido left alone in Africa while Aeneas, who was sort of her husband, sailed away to Italy because his destiny awaited him there. It seemed far too short a time before the teacher closed the book and said,

"We will resume Virgil tomorrow. Just now, we will move on to the study of Greek." Augustine put his head in his hands and groaned quietly.

* * *

"Augustine! Augustine, why are you still in bed? You must get up and go to school," called Monica from the corridor outside her son's bedroom. She knew that he hated his Greek lessons, but he was getting on so well with Latin literature and speeches that for many months now he had not begged her to take him out of school, as he used to do. She was surprised that he was still in his bedroom when it was time to go into Thagaste. She pushed back the curtain to the bedroom.

"Augustine?" He was still in bed. Even in the dim light Monica could see that something was wrong. The bedroom was warm but Augustine was shivering. Quickly, she pushed back the shutters from the window. In the daylight she could see that her son was very pale and his forehead was covered in sweat. She brushed back the hair from his forehead.

"Augustine? What's the matter?"

"Mother? Don't feel well. Cold."

Monica ran to the door. "Paula! Send out for the doctor!" she called to her slave. "Augustine is very sick."

The doctor came within an hour, but he did not bring good news.

"This is a very serious fever," he told Monica and Patrick. "I have seen it before. His temperature will reach a peak in a day or two. Then, one of two things will happen. Either the fever will break and he will get well, although he will still feel weak for a while. Or the fever will not break, and the illness will kill him. I must warn you, this is the more likely outcome. You should summon a priest."

Monica turned to Patrick, buried her head in his shoulder and wept for a few moments. Then she took a deep breath and pulled herself together.

"Thank you for your advice, Doctor. Our steward will see to your payment. I will go immediately to Father Crispus and ask him to come." She hurried away, leaving Patrick to see the doctor out, and returned half an hour later with Father Crispus, the local Christian priest. Crispus was a simple man, without much education, and whose Greek was no better than Augustine's, but he was kind and he did his best to teach the people of Thagaste about Jesus and the Bible. Now he spent the afternoon with Augustine, talking to him about Heaven and Hell and the sayings of Jesus. Augustine was very sick but he managed to confess his sins and declare his faith in Jesus through chattering teeth. The priest prayed over the boy, and turned to leave.

"B-baptized. I want to b-be b-baptized!" shivered Augustine. He looked from his mother to the priest. The two adults looked at each other, but Augustine couldn't tell what they were thinking.

11

"I'll talk to Father Crispus about it," said Monica, and they left the bedroom. Outside, Monica and the priest talked in hushed voices.

"Do you think it's a good idea, Father?"

"Yes, I think so. I realize that the boy doesn't have much understanding of the faith, but you wouldn't want him to die unbaptized, would you?"

"Of course not!" Monica replied. "But, what if he lives?" The priest nodded sympathetically. He knew why Monica was hesitating. Many people believed that sins committed after baptism were more serious than those committed before baptism. If Augustine lived, he would surely commit some sins in the future – perhaps God would not forgive them?[1] Crispus was no expert and he was not sure if Monica's belief was right. To check, though, would mean asking the bishop, who was out of town. Even if he sent him a letter the reply might not come for several days or weeks. Augustine did not have that long.

"I tell you what, we'll leave it for the time being. If Augustine gets worse and you think he won't make it, send someone to call me at any hour of the day or night. I will come immediately."

"Thank you, Father," said Monica, dabbing her eyes.

Augustine's fever got worse all evening. More than once Monica nearly sent for the priest, but then her son would seem to be more peaceful again and she

---

[1] This is a mistaken belief. Forgiveness of sins is a result of the work of Christ on the Cross not the good works of believers. When God forgives sinners he forgives their past sins and future sins.

hesitated. Finally, in the early hours of the morning, she was sure the end had come. Augustine had stopped moaning and shivering. Now he was convulsing, his legs and arms jerking around horribly. His breath came and went with a strange wheezing sound.

"Paula!" Monica screamed. "Send Marcus to get Father Crispus!" She sat holding her son by the shoulders for what felt like hours but was only a few minutes, until eventually he stopped thrashing about and started breathing normally. Monica's scream had woken Patrick, who came into his son's bedroom.

"Is he …?" Patrick couldn't finish the question, and Monica did not know how to answer him. They stared at their son for long minutes until, at last, his eyes flickered open.

"Mother? Father? Can I have some water?" Monica held a cup to Augustine's lips as he drank, and supported his head. His neck felt much cooler than before.

"Augustine, how do you feel?" she asked.

"I feel a little better," he replied. Then he smiled, turned over, and fell asleep. Monica slipped her arms around her husband and sobbed with relief.

"I think he's going to be alright! He's going to live, Patrick."

"Good, that's good. No need for any more tears, then," he chided her gently. They stood together for a long time, hugging and listening to their son's regular breathing, and they had forgotten all about sending for Father Crispus until there was a commotion from downstairs. Steps hurried up the stairs. Monica and Patrick slipped out into the corridor.

"Father Crispus, I'm so sorry! I thought Augustine was dying but now the fever has broken. I think he will be fine," Monica explained.

Father Crispus smiled broadly.

"That's a great relief! You don't have to apologize."

When Augustine awoke the next morning, weak but healthy, baptism was the last thing on his mind. Instead he only wanted to eat and eat and eat. Monica was just glad that her son was still alive, and Father Crispus never did write to the bishop, so the idea of Augustus' baptism was quietly forgotten.

Bad Company

Augustine recovered almost perfectly from his brush with death. The only reminder was a slight weakness in his lungs when he over-exerted himself. He continued to make progress at school. Although he still could not get the hang of Greek, his skill in Latin improved until he was the star pupil in Thagaste. He knew long passages of literature off by heart and was getting better and better at writing essays and making beautiful speeches. When he reached the age of fourteen, Patrick and Monica decided that it was time to send their son to the nearby town of Madaura to continue his studies.

Augustine was delighted. Madaura was only a few miles from Thagaste, but too far to travel home every day so he boarded in the larger town. This gave him much more freedom than he had ever had, without his watchful mother keeping an eye on him, or his brother Navigius telling tales on him if he did anything wrong. In Madaura, as long as he didn't do anything bad enough for the teachers to care about, he could live as he pleased. Augustine and his new friends visited the circus, where on festival days there were fights between bears and lions and hunting dogs, or gladiator battles. They slipped into the theatre and watched the new comic plays, repeating the dirty jokes to each other all the way home. In the evenings after lessons they played endless games, gambling food or possessions to make it more exciting. Augustine didn't have much luck at these games. He soon lost his small stash of possessions, and had to watch from the sidelines as the other boys played. If there was one thing Augustine hated, it was being left out. He visited his home in Thagaste regularly, and every time he returned to Madaura, just before he left the villa he would sneak into the cellar to steal some food, or wine, or olive oil, so that he could trade it in Madaura and join in the gambling again.

The best thing about Madaura was that there were no Greek lessons. Instead, Latin literature and rhetoric—the art of public speaking—made up the whole of the curriculum. The teachers at Augustine's new school liked to take their students on tours of the forum, pointing out the impressive statues of the gods and linking them to the passages of literature they were studying. They were not Christians, and spoke of the stories of the gods and heroes as if they were true, almost the way Father Crispus talked about the acts of Jesus. Augustine didn't really care. True or not, these ancient stories gave him the chance to show his skill at writing and speaking; he was able to work up so much emotion when he spoke that anyone hearing him could almost believe that, not only were they true, they had happened to him!

After Augustine had been at Madaura almost a year, there was an important speaking competition. This was the highlight of the school year and only the best students were invited to take part, while all the other boys were given the day off to listen to the speeches. Augustine, although he was one of the youngest students, was told that he would be taking part. The subject was "The Wrath of Juno". All of the competitors had to read the goddess Juno's angry speech from the first book of the *Aeneid*, put it into their own words, and recite it in front of the whole school.

Augustine stood trembling at the side of the stage, listening to the applause for the speech before his. What if no one applauded his speech? But he knew he had done his best, so taking a deep breath, he walked into the center of the stage and began:

"Why? Why, oh fates? Why am I so powerless that I cannot prevent this puny mortal, this mere man, this lump of flesh from crushing all my plans?" Caught up in the emotion of the speech, Augustine raged and shouted, drove his fingers through his hair in frustration and even let a few tears fall down his cheeks. When he had finished, there was silence. Still panting from the effort, Augustine looked at his audience. Why weren't they clapping? Didn't they like it? A moment later he was nearly blown backwards by the noise as the whole audience, students and teachers alike, rose to their feet, clapping, cheering and whistling. Augustine could see that he was not the only one who had been crying – many people in the audience also had tears running down their cheeks. Giddy with fluttery excitement, Augustine went to take his seat to listen to the rest of the speeches, although he hardly heard them.

It seemed like no time at all until the leader of the school walked on to the stage to announce the winner.

"Aurelius Augustine of Thagaste!" he cried. Augustine walked to the center of the stage with trembling legs, hardly able to believe it as the leader placed a wreath of leaves on his head. He was the youngest boy in the competition! Some of his competitors were seventeen or eighteen. His friends of his own age couldn't wait to congratulate him when they returned to their bedrooms at the end of the day.

"That was brilliant, Augustine! I've never heard anything like it!"

"How do you do it? It's incredible! You have a gift."

"You'll go far, Augustine! You'll probably end up working for the Roman Emperor himself, one day!"

Augustine fell asleep that night feeling that it had been the happiest day of his life. He felt special, as if he was going to achieve great things. He drifted off daydreaming about giving a speech to the Emperor, with the whole palace clapping and cheering. The following week, however, when he returned to his family's villa in Thagaste, his father, Patrick had news for Augustine that would dampen his daydreams:

"You know the harvest wasn't good this year, and taxes have gone up again. We'll all have to tighten our belts for a while. I'm sorry, Augustine, but I'm going to have to take you out of school."

* * *

Augustine kicked a stone along the dusty floor of the forum. He was so *bored*! Madaura was not a big city, not like Carthage or Rome, but it seemed like it, compared to Thagaste, with its pathetic little forum where second-rate lawyers fought unimportant court cases and stupid local politicians squabbled about the price of grain. One of those local politicians was his father. Augustine knew that one of the reasons his family was hard up was the cost of being involved in local politics. It wasn't Patrick's fault – it was the law that everyone of their social status had to serve in the local council—but it was just another reason to hate this stupid small town.

"Hey, Augustine!" It was his friend Iatanbaal, a year or two older him, and also the son of a town counsellor. Behind him trailed a group of his friends. Augustine had been spending more and more time with these lads, and less and less time out at his villa. He knew his mother didn't like it, she worried about him, but Patrick was the head of the household and he thought that his son, at fifteen, was old enough to look after himself.

"Hi Iatanbaal! What's up?"

"Nothing much. We'll see what turns up. Coming along?" Augustine accepted immediately, and fell in with the crew. He knew that Iatanbaal was the kind of friend his mother would hate him hanging around with, but he was the boy all the other teenagers wanted to be friends with. He was daring, and he seemed to know a lot about life. The group of boys moved through the darkening streets of Thagaste. Oil lamps started to come on in the houses they passed. They walked away from the town center towards the outskirts, where the houses were bigger and stood in orchards or fields. The branch of a pear tree hung over a wall, and one of the lads jumped up, trying to pick it. He missed twice and everyone laughed at him. Embarrassed, he changed his tack.

"I want those pears. Come on, who's with me?" A few of the boys said yes, others laughed.

"Yeah, why not?" said Iatanbaal. "Let's get them!"

"Yeah!" said Augustine, not wanting to be left out. He gave the first boy a boost on to the wall, then Iatanbaal helped him up. Soon the whole troupe of boys was sitting in the branches of the pear tree, grabbing the fruit. There was far too much to eat so they just took a bite or two from each pear, then threw them to the ground, or at each other. Soon they were sticky with juice and laughing like drunkards.

"Quick, quick! Someone's coming out of the house!"

Anxious not to be caught, the boys scrambled through the branches to the wall and dropped down into the street, where they scattered.

Augustine's villa was only a little further down the road so he ran for a few minutes, then slowed to a walk, making his way home as if nothing had happened. He couldn't shake a guilty feeling though, as he passed his family's vineyard. He hadn't been hungry. Those pears weren't as good as the grapes in this vineyard, which he could pick whenever he liked. He didn't even particularly like pears. They had destroyed the entire crop of that pear tree just for a laugh—but if he had said no the boys would have thought he was weak, and might not have wanted to hang around with him any more. He shrugged and entered the villa as quietly as he could, so that he could get to his room and remove his tunic before his mother noticed it was all covered in leaves and twigs, and stinking of pear juice.

For a couple of days Augustine hung around the villa and grounds. He played with his little sister and made himself useful by learning about accounting and estate management from Patrick. It wasn't as interesting as learning rhetoric, but it was better than nothing and might come in handy one day. Augustine and Patrick were on better terms now that Patrick had revealed that he had taken Augustine out of school at Madaura, not just because the household did not have enough money, but also so he could save up to send him somewhere better – to university in Carthage, the most important city in Africa!

On Sunday Augustine went with his mother and his brother and sisters to church. Since he had returned from Madaura, Augustine had began to hang around at the back of the church with other bored teenage boys. The bishop droned on about something or other, but Augustine and his friends played dice and knucklebones. Iatanbaal and a few of the others were not present because they were pagans, but Augustine and the other boys in church had been brought up as Christians. He assumed that they would probably get baptized some day, when they were old and boring, but for now they just saw church as a place to chat and gamble.

"I'm going to see Iatanbaal and the others after church," said one of the boys. "Want to come?" Augustine hesitated for a moment. "Unless you have to hold your mother's hand on the way home!" the boy quipped. The others sniggered.

"Sure," said Augustine, "I'll come."

Being near the back, Augustine and his friends were out of the door like a shot after the service. Monica often stopped to talk to the priest or bishop, so she was used to her teenaged son leaving without her. Round the back of the forum, Iatanbaal and his crew waited, kicking a ball around.

"Here come the Christian boys! Feeling all holy and blessed, are you? You don't know what you're missing, you Christians. You've probably never even had a girl, have you?" Some of the other boys from the church protested, but Iatanbaal could tell from Augustine's blush that his dig had hit home. He laughed.

"Don't worry about it, Augustine, you've got to start somewhere. Let's go and see about it just now." The group traipsed off to a back street that some of the older boys knew, and were long gone before Monica, wondering anxiously what her son was up to, emerged from the church.

Love, but no Marriage

Patrick ducked his head as a slave poured a bucket of hot water over him. The baths were very full because it was one of the days when entry was free, so Patrick had decided to take Augustine there. He was still trying to save money whenever he could. Monica was worried about her son, who stayed in town till all hours, keeping company with boys who had bad reputations. She'd been the one to suggest that he spend some time with Augustine, so here they were. Patrick had recently given up his pagan faith and become a catechumen, a beginner in Christianity. Monica, who was delighted that her years of prayers for her husband had paid off, now hoped that the same openness to God might rub off on Augustine.

Patrick looked around the baths trying to see Augustine, who had taken longer to undress and come through than he had. At first he couldn't see him anywhere, then suddenly he realized that the well-built young man at the other side of the pool was his son. He hadn't even recognized him! It had been a long time since he had seen Augustine naked and he had been looking around for a skinny young boy who didn't exist any more. The Augustine who stood in front of him now could not be mistaken for a child any more. He looked like a full-grown man. Patrick laughed and slapped his thigh in happy surprise, sending a splash of water on to the mosaic floor of the bathhouse, and startling the slave who was scrubbing his back.

Back at the villa, Monica wanted to know how Patrick's trip to the baths with Augustine had gone.

"Extremely well! In fact, I think I might crack open the new wine to celebrate." Monica smiled, wondering what could have made Patrick so happy. Her husband continued: "It won't be that long until we're having grandchildren—our son has grown up to be a man!"

"Oh dear!" said Monica. "I mean, it's wonderful that he's growing up, but I worry about what he gets up to. He's not a little boy any more. Do you think he's already…? What if he gets some girl into trouble or, God forbid, is attacked by a jealous husband?"

"Calm yourself, woman," replied Patrick. "He's a bright boy, I'm sure he knows what's what and can take care of himself. We should be celebrating!"

Monica tried to be happy for her husband's sake, but she could not calm her fears about Augustine's behavior. She decided to have a serious talk with him. Slipping into his bedroom late one morning, when Augustine had just woken up after another night out, she sat down on the bed and took her son's hand.

"Augustine, I want to talk to you. You're not a boy any more, you're a man. As a man, there are some things I want you to bear in mind." Augustine frowned, but he did not withdraw his hand.

"Firstly, although I expect you want to try everything all at once, remember that you have your whole life. 'There is a time for everything, and a season for every activity under the heavens.'[1] Please don't get involved with girls now." Her son squirmed and blushed. "Mother, you don't have to tell me these things, I'm fine, really."

"I feel that I must, Augustine, because you keep such bad company, and stay out late, and drink. You are getting a bad reputation. I don't want you to think that you have to live up to it! Don't have sex before you get married."

Augustine almost groaned. This was so embarrassing!

"Secondly," Monica continued, "if you do slip up and lose your self control, please, *please* make sure that you never get involved with a married woman![2] You would bring so much shame on your family, and put yourself in danger from the law, too."

"Alright, Mother, alright!" cried Augustine, pulling his hand away. "You don't need to say any more." Monica smiled and left her son to get up and dressed.

Augustine, alone, shook his head. That had been so awkward! He hoped Monica would never bring the

---

[1] Ecclesiastes 3:1 (NIV)

[2] The advice about married women is taken straight from what Monica really said in Confessions II.iii (7)

subject up again. He supposed it was a mother's role to have this sort of talk with her children and, as a young man, it was his role to completely ignore her. After all, everyone knew that this chastity stuff was for girls; it didn't really apply to boys. At least she hadn't asked him if he had already done anything like that – he hated lying to his mother.

* * *

A few weeks later, when Augustine was out of the house, Monica asked Patrick if she could speak to him. They sat in the courtyard at the center of their villa, shaded from the hot sun by an orange tree.

"What is worrying you now? I thought you talked to the boy," Patrick said.

"I did, but I don't think he took me seriously. I have heard that Augustine and his friends have been stealing and vandalizing, and visiting that street, you know, the one where the prostitutes work." Patrick did know it. His own father, a pagan, had taken him to that street for the first time when he was about Augustine's age.

"You shouldn't listen to gossip, Monica. I'm sure he's just doing the things that all the boys his age are doing." Monica was stung by the word "gossip". Normally she avoided gossip because it was often unfair and damaging, but in the case of her son she did listen to all the tales she could because she was so anxious about his behavior.

"I know it might be exaggerated," she said, "and I shouldn't listen to every story I hear. But there must be some truth in it, Patrick! I'm so worried he's going astray." Patrick stroked his wife's back. Brought up a pagan, he did not really think it was a problem if young men were a bit wild, as long as they settled down later. He knew that his wife thought differently, though. She respected the laws of God about keeping your body pure and saving yourself for marriage.

"Well, what would you like to do then? If I speak to him or punish him it probably won't have much effect. Do you think it's time to find Augustine a wife?" Monica thought for a long time before she answered.

"That would solve the problem, of course, and some of his friends from school are already married. But if he marries now…" Patrick understood what was bothering his wife. Augustine was so promising. He could easily end up in the imperial civil service, here in Africa or even in another part of the empire, but that would be harder if he was married to a simple local girl.

"You'd prefer to wait until he's made a name for himself, wouldn't you?" Patrick said. "Then we can arrange a really good marriage with a girl from a rich family, maybe with connections in Italy; a marriage that would give his career a big boost."

"Yes," said Monica, "exactly. Maybe I'm being over-ambitious for him, but the last thing I want to do now is hold him back."

"So, no marriage for now," said Patrick. "It's agreed."

"But what are we going to do about his terrible behavior?" asked Monica.

"I don't think you need to worry about that," reassured Patrick. "I've saved up a lot of money, and the next harvest looks like it will be good. I'll get a loan from Romanianus on the strength of it, and Augustine will be in Carthage within a month or two. Once he has his studies to occupy him again he won't have time for any wild living."

* * *

Carthage was amazing. It was huge, the biggest city in Africa. It was rich; the public baths had vast vaulted ceilings that soared up to heaven, and every surface was covered in marble or mosaic art. In the broad streets citizens strode confidently in brightly colored clothes. Their billowing cloaks had complicated pictures embroidered on them, some in gold thread.

"What's that smell?" Augustine asked the slave who accompanied him, carrying his luggage.

The slave did not know, but as Augustine continued his exploration and reached the enormous, busy harbour, the scent was blown off the water and hit him full in the face. It was the sea!

"I didn't know the sea had a smell!" he cried. Augustine could have stayed all day watching the waves slapping at the hulls of the ships, the dark blue waters rolling and sliding, always changing – but there was so much else to see!

The social life, too, was different from Thagaste or even Madaura. There were thousands of young men studying here, all old enough to have no-one checking up on them, but young enough to go a little crazy with the new-found freedom. There were clubs and secret societies. Some followed mysterious religions, while others were dedicated to nothing more than vandalism and picking on new students. There were theatres with plays fresh out of Rome and circuses with much better gladiator and animal fights than in Madaura. And there were girls, so many girls! Augustine followed his mother's advice to find a church in Carthage and attend it regularly, but mainly because he had quickly discovered from the other students that a lot of girls also attended the church. Now instead of playing knucklebones with his teenage friends at the back of the church he spent his time chatting up girls. Some of them wanted nothing to do with him, and told him to stop talking to them when they were listening to the sermon. Other girls came with their parents or a household slave who made sure that boys did not pester them. There were always some, though, who were on their own, or in small groups, or who had slaves that were easy to bribe. Those were the ones who were worth talking to.

Augustine fell in love. Again and again, he fell in love. Every week seemed to bring a new love affair. In Thagaste his encounters with girls had only been physical, they had not affected his emotions. Now, at seventeen, he felt the fear of being turned down, the pain of being dumped by a girl, the shame of being laughed at by her friends. It was like being in the plays

Augustine loved at the theatre. His head swam with all the love affairs until he could not even keep up with them himself. His friends didn't even try to remember who Augustine was going out with this week.

So Patrick's assurance about Carthage solving the problem with Augustine's behavior turned out to be wrong. Back in Thagaste, Monica would hear about the life her son was living from time to time, when a friend or relative had visited the city, and it broke her heart. She spent more and more of her prayer time talking to God about it. But Patrick had been right about one thing—Augustine *was* busy with his studies. Despite his hectic personal life, he did not neglect his learning. He loved the literature he was given to study. In Thagaste and Madaura they had only studied the same few authors over and over again. Now he was introduced to dozens more. He was also able to read more books by his favorite authors. There was a library, and books were sold in the marketplace and on street corners. Some of the books were history, some were legal speeches, some were plays or poems, but as well as all this there were also excellent books on philosophy. Augustine had no idea, but these books of philosophy were going to change his life.

Looking for Wisdom

In a sunny courtyard a couple of students were playing at dice for coppers. In the corner, not far from them, another young man was trying to write poetry, but he wasn't getting very far because he kept watching the game or joining in with the conversation. Eventually he gave up, put his wax tablet and stylus down, and came over to sit with his friends.

"Where's Augustine these days?" he asked. "I haven't seen him in ages. Is he back in Thagaste?" The winner gathered up his latest handful of coins and added them to his pile, which was becoming considerably bigger than his friend's.

"No, I don't think so, Nebridius. I think he's here in Carthage."

"I haven't seen much of him either," said the other friend, counting his shrinking pile of coins. "He's really keeping himself to himself. Do you think it's because of his father?" Augustine's father had died quite suddenly the year before, not long after Augustine had started his studies in Carthage. Naturally, Augustine had spent quite a lot of time in Thagaste making sure his family and the estate were all right; that was his duty as one of the sons.

"I suppose it could be," Nebridius said, "but they were never very close. It's not like Augustine to brood on his own. He would want to spend time with us, his friends, if he were upset about his father's death." Nebridius stood up. "I'll go and check if he's okay. I'm getting nowhere with this piece of poetry, anyway. Where is he living these days?" One of the others supplied directions, and Nebridius said goodbye and walked out of the courtyard.

* * *

Nebridius strolled slowly through the streets of Carthage. It was the middle of the morning, but not very hot yet. He walked towards the shore, to the part of town where Augustine lived. As he walked, he thought about his friend. They had come to know each other as students in Carthage, although their backgrounds were quite different. Like many students, Augustine had ambition—he had to excel. His family were no doubt hoping that he would make a great career as a lawyer or a civil servant, and win honors that were not available in a small, backwater town like Thagaste. Nebridius, on the other hand, came from a family that had plenty of money and status, so he had no need to work hard to win honors and promotions. He studied to make himself a well-educated gentleman, and because he enjoyed it.

Not everyone had that luxury. However, despite the difference in their social status, Nebridius had come to think of Augustine as a good friend. He hoped there was nothing wrong.

After asking a few neighbors, Nebridius managed to find Augustine's lodgings. He was surprised when the door was opened by a pretty girl. Her clothes weren't fancy but she didn't look like a slave or a servant. The girl asked who Nebridius was, then went to call Augustine. Nebridius waited in the hallway until Augustine came.

"Nebridius! It's so good to see you! It feels like I haven't seen you in weeks."

"You haven't, actually," replied Nebridius. "That's why I thought I should come round."

"Oh," said Augustine. "Yes, you're right. I'm sorry. Listen, let's go out to that nice Greek wine shop in the square and we'll catch up." He went back into the apartment to pick up his cloak and purse, and Nebridius caught sight of him giving a quick kiss goodbye to the girl who had opened the door.

On the way to the wine shop they talked about nothing in particular; Augustine mentioned the latest plays he had seen and Nebridius described the piece of poetry he was struggling to write. When they reached the wine shop, though, and the chilled wine was set down in front of them, Augustine opened up.

"I'm sorry I've been out of touch. I've been busy with my studies of course, and I've been doing a bit of teaching as well, to help with money, but—well, you met the real reason back at the apartment."

"The girl?"

"Yes. I've been seeing her for a few months. I met her in church not long after I came back to Carthage after my father's death. She was a great comfort to me, so understanding. One thing led to another and we started going out, you know how it is." Nebridius nodded. One thing always seemed to lead to another with Augustine, who usually had more girlfriends in a month than Nebridius had had in his entire life.

"Anyway," Augustine went on, pouring more cool wine, "a couple of weeks ago she moved in with me." Nebridius raised an eyebrow. *This* had never happened before. "It's been so nice, having a woman in the house," said Augustine, "I suppose I've just forgotten to go out and meet people!" Nebridius raised his glass.

"Well, let us drink to her, then. Here's to…"

"Una."

"Here's to Una! She must be a special young lady, if she can hold on to Augustine for more than a few weeks!" Nebridius laughed. Augustine laughed too, but looking a bit sheepish he said, "She is quite special. Everything up to now has just been flings, but I feel like I could settle down with her. I'm really serious about her."

"Are you going to marry her?" Nebridius asked.

"What? No!" replied Augustine. "She's just a simple girl from Carthage. She's got no connections, no family money. My ambitions lie a bit higher than that! No, we'll just live together." Nebridius' smile faded a little. He was glad that Augustine had turned his back on his crazy love affairs, but this wasn't much better. Still, he could understand someone in Augustine's position putting his ambition before his relationship, so he just clasped his friend's arm and said, "I hope you'll be very happy with her."

The two young men chatted for a while longer about their classes, their friends, and the revolt that had taken place in nearby Mauritania. But soon it was midday, the sun was blazing down, and it was time for them to return to their lodgings. Augustine was happy as he walked back to his apartment. It had been good to catch up with Nebridius—good to get out of the apartment, too, even though he enjoyed spending time with Una. There was just one thing that was spoiling his mood, though—something that he did not want to reveal to his friends yet: a few days earlier, Una had told him that she was pregnant.

Later that day, when they had eaten and Una was tidying up, Augustine decided to get down to some work. The university syllabus covered all kinds of different writing and speaking to prepare young men for a life as teachers, magistrates or civil servants. Having a good style in Latin was the most important skill to be learned, so students were expected to study classic works by Roman authors. Augustine picked up the next book he was going to study. It was called

Hortensius and was a book of philosophy by the very famous writer Cicero, who had died more than three hundred years earlier. Augustine settled himself down on the couch and began reading. He could never have imagined what would happen next.

Within a few hours, Augustine was not paying any attention at all to the Latin style in the book, which was what he was supposed to be studying. Instead, his mind was reeling with the ideas Cicero had written about. Cicero said that true happiness was found in wisdom, not in pleasures of the body like eating, drinking and sex. Human beings are not animals, so it is the part that makes them different from animals that they should spend their lives on: the mind and the soul.

Augustine felt like he had been living in a stuffy room and someone had just thrown open a window. The fresh air of Cicero's ideas blew away all the cobwebs of his assumptions about life. He realized that up until now he had been using his mind to serve his body, and had completely ignored his soul. That was the wrong way round! The body, which is temporary, should actually serve the soul, which lasts forever. Without realizing it, Augustine had come to a crossroads in his life; and without hesitation, as if it had always been his destiny, he chose the path that led to wisdom.

After he finished reading *Hortensius*, Augustine was itching to know more. He felt as if his spirit had been starved while he had frittered his time away on clever talk, women, and career ambitions. The ideas in *Hortensius* about focussing on the part of us that makes us truly human, the part that is closest to God, reminded him of things he had learnt when he was younger, back when he had still paid attention in church: "God made human beings that resembled Him"; "put to death your earthly desires"; "set your minds on things above". Phrases like these came floating up out of his brain where he had forgotten them for so long. He decided that the next day he would go to a nearby church and read their Bible. That must be where wisdom could be found.

The Bible was a big disappointment. Augustine was still awful at Greek so he tried reading the Latin translation of the Bible, but it seemed as if the people who had translated it weren't much better at Greek than he was. The Latin was terrible! Augustine was used to the best Latin writing that existed, and this had to be some of the worst. But it wasn't just the style that put him off, it was the content, too. He had come looking for wisdom and instead he had found stories about animals being sacrificed, and men marrying more than one wife. As a gifted student at Carthage, who already taught younger students, Augustine did not even consider approaching a priest or an older Christian to get help understanding the Bible. Instead he closed the book, and decided that wherever wisdom was to be found, it was not here.

Still, the nagging itch was there, telling him, as Cicero said, to "love and seek and pursue" wisdom.

He read more books of philosophy, and started paying more attention to astrologers, in case that was where the truth lay. One day, as he was reading a book of philosophy in the shade of a tree, another student stopped and smiled at him.

"I always see you reading philosophy! And your friends tell me you like to talk about the true meaning of life. Would I be right in thinking that you're a man in search of the truth?" he asked. Augustine put his book down.

"I certainly am. But where can true wisdom be found? If I knew, I'd have found it by now!" Augustine expected the young man to shrug his shoulders and say, "who knows?" like most of his friends did, but he didn't. Instead he looked intensely at Augustine, still smiling, and said, "The truth is there, for those who are willing to look for it. There are secrets of the universe just waiting to be revealed to anyone who is truly willing to learn. Are you really a fellow-traveller on the road to truth?"

"I am," said Augustine, "or at least, I'd like to be."

"Then meet me here tonight at dusk, and I'll take you to meet some people who have all the answers about God, the universe, even the purpose of life. I'll take you to meet the Manichees."

Divided Loyalties

Monica wept as she read the letter from her son. He was writing to tell her that he had finished his studies in Carthage and had decided to return to his hometown, Thagaste, to become a teacher. This was not what was making Monica cry however. Augustine would also be bringing his girlfriend with him, and their baby son, who was called Adeodatus, meaning 'given by God'. Monica had mixed feelings about this. It was wonderful to have her first grandson, but she wished her son had not started living with a woman he was not married to. She knew it was considered normal in Carthage, but it was still wrong. But what was making Monica cry was what she had heard from friends who had been to Carthage: Augustine had become a Manichee. He had turned his back on Jesus and the Bible and was instead following an illegal, false religion. That, she could not put up with. She felt that she could not let him live in her household now he was a Manichee. She would have to shut her own son out of the house!

Augustine was shocked when he reached Thagaste with his family and his belongings, only to be told that he was not welcome in his own house. But his new Manichee friends had explained to him that Christians were prejudiced and ignorant. They did not understand the real truth. Augustine, however, thought his mother would eventually open her mind to the new and exciting things he was learning once he had had the chance to talk to her. In the meantime, he went to stay with Romanianus, a friend of his family who had often helped them out and had even loaned his father the money to send him to Carthage in the first place. Romanianus was also a Manichee now, after talking to Augustine about it in Carthage. So were Augustine's other friends back in Carthage, including Nebridius. Augustine had spent years of school and university studying the art of making persuasive arguments, and people found it hard to stand up to him when he set his mind to convince them of something. He was sure his mother would come round to Manichaeism in time.

In fact, Monica seemed to come round much sooner than he thought. Only a few weeks after his return to Thagaste, Augustine received news that his mother would like him and his family to move in with her and his brother and sister. Romanianus was glad to see Augustine and his mother getting on again, so he didn't mind at all. Monica was waiting for her son at the door of the villa.

"Welcome back, Augustine," she said. "Welcome, Una. And this must be Adeodatus! Let me hold him!" Augustine smiled as his mother cooed over her baby grandson. It felt good to be back home. Later, when Una was feeding the baby in another room, he sat with Monica in the courtyard and asked why she had changed her mind.

"I had a dream—a dream which I believe was from God," she replied. Augustine leaned forward, interested. Monica went on, "I dreamed that you and I were standing on a huge ruler, but we were at different places on the ruler, far apart. A voice said to me, 'Where you are, he will also be.' I'm sure it meant that you will one day return to the church, to the truth."

Augustine scoffed. He respected his mother, but she must be wrong about this dream. After all, wasn't finding out the truth the reason he had joined the Manichees? Taking his mother's hand and smiling his most persuasive smile, Augustine said, "So we will both end up in the same place. Are you sure the voice didn't mean that one day, *you* will see the truth, and we will both be Manichees?"

Monica wasn't so easily persuaded.

"No, Augustine. It said that where *I* am, *you* will be some day. And I will pray for you every day until it happens." Augustine was annoyed by his mother's certainty. He was a very well educated man, now, but she still thought she knew better than him! However, he was glad that they were friends again and that she had invited him home, so he just shook his head, kissed her, and went to check how Una and little Adeodatus were getting on.

Monica watched her son as he walked into the house. He was a grown man now, and thought he knew so much, but to her he seemed so lost, looking for the truth in places where it couldn't be found. She knew she just had to be patient. She had spoken to a bishop about Augustine being a Manichee, before she had the dream about the ruler, and he had also reassured her.

"I was brought up a Manichee," he told her, "and I spent a lot of my younger life copying out their sacred books. In the end I realized that their 'truth' was nonsense—it just doesn't fit with reality and logic. Augustine is an intelligent man. As he learns more about what Manichees really believe, he will realize this, too."

Monica trusted in the bishop's words, and more than that she trusted in the dream, which she believed was from God. However, she knew that the most important thing of all was to take the problem to God and ask him to deal with it. So once again, as she did every day, Monica prayed for her son.

* * *

Augustine very much enjoyed being back in Thagaste —more than he had expected, in fact. Of course, the theatre and circus events were much less impressive in a small town, and were held less often, but since becoming a Manichee he had tried to leave these "earthly" pleasures behind him, so it didn't matter that much. What he really enjoyed, when he had finished teaching for the day, was spending time with his friends and talking about the things that interested them. They discussed literature, philosophy and especially the ideas of the prophet Mani. All of them were only beginners in the faith, so they were not allowed to hear the whole of the secret truth yet, but what they already knew was exciting and different.

"It makes so much sense!" Augustine would often exclaim. "The idea that the whole universe is divided into good and evil, and the good forces fight against the evil ones. It explains so much! That's why we so often do bad things even though we want to be good—it's the particles of darkness inside us that are responsible, not our true selves. All we have to do is find out how to remove the particles of darkness so that our souls can be good—and in time the Manichees will teach us this."

"You're right, Augustine," his friends agreed. "The more we learn the secret truth, the better our lives will be."

There was one friend in particular that Augustine loved spending time with. He was a young man of his own age, called Amatus. Although they had been to school together in Thagaste, Amatus had not studied at Carthage so the two men did not know each other especially well. However, when Augustine returned to Thagaste a few years older, and bumped into his schoolmate again, they discovered that they had more in common than they ever expected. More than that, they saw things the same way, they shared the same sense of humor, and they just seemed to understand each other as they had never been understood before. Very soon Augustine and Amatus became best friends, spending all of their free time together.

Amatus was from a Christian family, like Augustine, but as Augustine explained to him about Manichee beliefs and how exciting they were, Amatus started to share his enthusiasm. Soon he was calling himself a Manichee too, like the rest of Augustine's friends. Augustine was pleased to see how many of his friends had started following the secret wisdom of the Manichees, but he was especially happy about Amatus because it was another thing they had in common. The two of them thought so much alike that it sometimes felt to Augustine as if he was talking to a twin soul. Opening his heart to Amatus about anything and everything was his greatest pleasure in life. All the fun and distractions of Carthage seemed totally unnecessary.

Augustine had been back in Thagaste almost a year, and had established an excellent reputation as a teacher of Latin, when Amatus was suddenly taken ill. It was a dangerous fever. As soon as Augustine heard, he cancelled all of his classes and rushed to Amatus' house. Amatus was unconscious, pale and sweating. His cheeks were sunken and his eye sockets looked hollow. The life seemed to be draining away from him. Augustine grasped his hand.

"How long has he been like this?" he asked the doctor who was attending.

"He has been unconscious now for almost twenty-four hours. I am doing everything I can, but there is a real chance he won't pull through." Augustine brushed tears from his eyes and tried to remain positive.

"But there is a good chance he will make it?" he asked.

"He may, certainly he may," the doctor replied. "He is young and strong. But I am not confident. The boy's mother has gone to fetch the priest, and I cannot tell her that she is wrong to do so."

"A priest?" scoffed Augustine. "Amatus doesn't believe in those old Hebrew superstitions! He is a follower of the true light—a Manichee, like me!"

The doctor shrugged. It was not his job to get involved in religious arguments. Preventing death was his concern, not preaching about what happened after death. He turned to Amatus again and took his pulse. Augustine saw that his friend's arm trembled as the doctor held it. Amatus' whole body was shivering slightly, despite the oppressive African heat. Sweat ran down his pale forehead and stained the thin sheet that covered him. Holding his friend's other hand, Augustine prayed to the Light not to let the forces of Darkness take his friend.

Soon Amatus' mother returned with the priest. The baptism was carried out quickly and without fuss; the priest said some prayers and poured a little water over the sick man's head. Amatus' mother thanked the priest, tears running down her cheeks.

"Thank you, Father. It gives me comfort to know that, even if his body is in danger, at least his soul is safe." Augustine shook his head at her ridiculous superstition, but was too polite to say anything.

Augustine stayed at Amatus' house that night. A couple of times during the night a servant came through to his room to tell him that Amatus might be about to die, but both times, after sweating and moaning, he became quiet again. In the morning, Augustine awoke to the wonderful news that Amatus was conscious, and talking! Augustine rushed through to Amatus' bedroom, a huge smile of relief on his face. Amatus was too weak to sit up but he was talking quietly to his mother and other relatives. His mother kept brushing away her tears without even noticing she was crying. Every so often a little sob of joy would escape her as she stroked her son's hair.

Eventually, when his brothers, sisters and aunts had finished telling Amatus how relieved they were, Augustine got a chance to talk to him alone. They didn't joke together as they usually did, because Amatus was so weak, but Augustine told him how wonderful it was to see him awake again.

"We had almost given you up for dead!" he said. "Would you believe, your mother even had you baptized while you were unconscious? What a ridiculous thing to do, as if a wet forehead is going to have any effect against the forces of darkness!"

"Don't joke, Augustine!" Amatus said. His voice was weak, but his tone was surprisingly firm. "I realize now that only Jesus can save me. I thought it was fun to dabble in this exotic new religion, but when it comes to life or death—and life after death—my trust is in Jesus. It took this illness to make me see that." Amatus finished his heartfelt speech and started coughing, which started him off shivering again. His mother and the doctor rushed in, and started fussing over him until he was settled.

Augustine hovered around in the back of the room, confused by Amatus' words. Amatus was closer to him than a brother. How could he change his opinion on this important issue? He saw that Amatus was falling asleep, which was probably the best thing for him. After his disturbed night and all the worry about his friend, sleep seemed like a good idea for Augustine, too. He decided to go back to his family home, where he could have a nap and a wash. He kissed the sleeping Amatus goodbye, and left.

Augustine slept longer than he intended. He was still sleeping that afternoon when a messenger came to the door. A slave came to wake him so that he could be given the messenger's news: The fever had returned; Amatus was dead.

Running Away

Thagaste without Amatus was torture for Augustine. Everywhere he went reminded him of his friend, because they had been there together. Everything he enjoyed doing was something they had enjoyed doing together. Even spending time with his other friends was no comfort, because at every moment he expected Amatus to turn up and join them, then remembered that he never would again. Una and Monica tried to comfort him, but whatever Augustine did to take his mind off Amatus just didn't work.

"I can't stay here," he told Una. "We have to go back to Carthage."

Life back in Carthage went on as fast as ever, and although Augustine still missed Amatus, there was much more to take his mind off it. And there was all the news! Thagaste was so slow to hear about what was happening in the wider Empire, but here in Carthage news travelled much faster. All the talk was about the barbarians called Goths, who had crossed the great River Danube and started to invade the Roman Empire.

The Emperor had sent forces to attack them, including the general Maximus who had served in Africa a few years earlier. The rumor was that the Goths were being pushed into Roman territory by an even more barbaric race at their backs, the Huns, but no one knew any more than that. The news of revolts and Barbarian invasions made it sound like the Roman Empire was fraying at the edges, but life in comfortable, exciting Carthage went on as usual.

Augustine went back to teaching, this time in the center of a big city, not a small town. He had many pupils, most of them rich, because Romanianus had recommended him widely. Romanianus' own sons attended his classes, as did his young relative Alypius, who soon became part of Augustine's group of friends. Like most of Augustine's friends, he also soon became a Manichee. Augustine himself, though, was starting to have his doubts.

As the years and months passed, and Augustine continued to attend the Manichees' meetings, he began to copy out their sacred books and was let into more and more of their secret knowledge. At first it was exciting, and he loved to use Manichee arguments to try to prove that Christians were wrong about God.

"If God made the soul, how can it sin?" he would ask them. "Surely, if God is good, anything that comes from God must be good!" Then he would explain that the Manichees taught that a person has two souls—a good one that is a part of God, and the bad one that is a part of the forces of darkness. Augustine thought this was a good explanation for why people can do both good things and bad things, and also explained why there were both good and bad things in the world.

But as he learned more, his belief in Manichee teachings started to be strained. As a junior Manichee he had to help to buy and prepare food for the Elect, the great leaders of the faith who lived quiet lives, never married, and ate only certain kinds of vegetables. He was surprised when he learned that, by eating the vegetables, the Elect released particles of light that could then travel back to God. He was even more surprised when it was explained to him that these light particles were stored in the moon, causing it to become full, then transported to the sun, so that the moon became empty again. Augustine had studied science, including astronomy, and he knew that the moon only appeared to be full or empty, but it was always the same size.

Then there were eclipses. The Manichees said that they were caused by divine beings sometimes not wanting to look at the great battle between good and evil that was being fought on earth, but astronomers were able to predict exactly when eclipses would happen based on facts about the sun, moon and earth. Could both of these things be true? Augustine was very confused. He wanted Manichaeism to be true because it explained that sinning was not his fault, and because he had by now devoted years of his life to the religion, but as a philosopher he could not believe in something that could be proved false.

"It just doesn't seem to make sense," he said to some of his Manichee friends. "Is there something I am not seeing?" His friends shrugged and told him to talk to the Elect. The Elect, who were thin and foreign and strange looking, were not able to reassure him either. They knew far less about science than he did, so they could not answer his questions. Many times the name of Faustus was mentioned:

"Wait for Faustus. When he comes he will explain everything."

"Faustus is a very wise man. You must put your questions to him."

"These are great mysteries—but perhaps Faustus will be able to shine blessed light on them, when he is next in Africa."

Augustine started to be eager to meet this Faustus, a Manichee bishop who was a great missionary and travelled far and wide. He put aside his doubts for the time being and tried to be patient. Meanwhile, he had plenty to occupy him. As well as teaching all of his students, he spent time composing poems and making speeches for competitions, not only to win money but also to get the attention of important men who might be able to help him in his career. In Carthage, people came and went all the time from other parts of the Roman Empire, and it was beginning to bother Augustine that he had never left Africa. To tell the truth he was beginning to get a little tired of Carthage, after years and years of teaching the same things. His ambitions, forgotten for a few years after reading *Hortensius*, were starting to rub at him again.

One day, after years of waiting, he heard the news he had been waiting for: "Faustus is here! He has arrived in Carthage!" Augustine could not wait to meet him and ask him all his questions. Although he was not usually patient to learn from other people, because he was so intelligent and educated himself, he thought that the great Faustus must be a suitable teacher for him. Everyone said that Faustus knew everything about the Manichee faith!

First of all Faustus had to meet with the other members of the Elect, of course, and to appear at the secret Manichee meetings. Augustine was very impressed with his wise teaching and his clever speeches, but he was disappointed that there was no opportunity to ask questions or have a discussion. After Faustus had been in Carthage for a few weeks, however, he had more free time and Augustine and his friends got a chance to talk to him properly. At last Augustine was able to ask him all the important questions!

"How can it be that the moon is literally filled up with particles of light, then emptied, when science shows that it is always the same size? Why does the moon's size and shape change as it gets filled up, but the sun stays the same?"

Faustus smiled in amazement at so many intelligent questions.

"You certainly have an inquiring mind, young Augustine!" he said. "As for myself, I don't know much about science. I don't pretend to understand the mysterious workings of the heavenly bodies such as the sun and the moon. I content myself with the books written by the great prophet Mani, who has shown us the truth about how to serve the light and oppose the darkness." Augustine's hopes sank within him. If even the great Faustus could not explain the problems he had found in Manichee beliefs, who could?

Augustine became friends with Faustus, and they had many interesting conversations about literature, especially books that Augustine recommended to Faustus, who had not had a very good education. Whenever Augustine tried to bring up scientific or philosophical problems, though, Faustus always refused to get involved.

"I won't come up with opinions about things I don't understand, Augustine," he always said, "for that would be arrogance and foolishness." After Augustine had turned his back on Christianity he had believed that Manichaeism offered all the answers. Now it looked as if Manichaeism might be false, too. He began to wonder if anyone really knew the truth about spiritual things. There didn't seem to be any promising alternatives. Augustine still attended Manichee meetings but in his heart he had given up on religion, at least for the time being. Instead, he started to throw his energy into his career. He set his sights on Rome.

Carthage was an important city in the Roman Empire, and the politicians who ruled it were important men, with connections in other cities, including Rome. Augustine already had contact with them because he taught some of their sons, but now he made more of an effort to call on these men to pay his respects. Whenever he was invited to their houses he made the greatest effort to make a good impression by talking about philosophy and rhetoric, using all his skill as a public speaker. Augustine was determined to make good connections so that he could move to Rome as a teacher.

Everyone told him that students in Rome were well behaved. In fact, the City Perfect of Rome checked to see that they were studying and not attending too many parties! It sounded wonderful, compared to the students in Carthage who caused havoc and half the time could not be bothered to study at all. Then there were the wages—much higher in Rome, he had heard. Most of all, there were the opportunities. Important politicians might come to Carthage for a few years, but many of them had permanent houses in Rome. There would be so many more opportunities for Augustine to rise to an important position himself—maybe become rich and famous! Finally, there was Alypius, who had quickly become one of Augustine's best friends. He had already used his excellent family connections to move to Rome to work as a lawyer.

Soon Augustine felt that he had all the support and financial backing that he needed to make the big move to Rome. His first time out of Africa! His first chance to see the city that founded the whole Roman Empire! At the age of twenty-nine he was finally going to launch his international career. There was only one problem: Monica.

As soon as Augustine's mother heard that her son was planning to sail for Rome she rushed to Carthage. Monica often visited her son, and Augustine often went to visit her in Thagaste, for they were very fond of each other, but this time it was different. She refused to leave Augustine alone so that he could not leave her and go to Italy.

"Please, Augustine," she begged, "promise me that you won't go away and leave us. Rome is so far away, and the sea is so dangerous! Stay with me here in Africa! Or at least wait a year or two until your sisters are old enough to marry and I can come with you." Augustine felt very uncomfortable. He had made up his mind that he was going to Rome but he could not bring himself to tell his mother that, not when she was crying and hugging him. So he lied to her.

"Don't worry, Mother, I'll stay here if you insist." Monica seemed a little happier after he reassured her, but Augustine could tell that she did not completely trust him—and nor should she. Whenever he was away from his home without her, he was making arrangements and putting plans in place to sail to Rome. Eventually the day came. His ship was to sail that night. Augustine knew there was no way he could go to the harbour at that time of night without Monica knowing exactly what was going on. So he lied again.

"I have a friend who is sailing to Italy in the morning," he told her. "He's a very dear friend and I want to spend every possible minute with him before he goes, since I may not see him for years afterwards—so don't worry if I don't come home tonight. Why don't you visit that shrine of Cyprian that you mentioned, and I'll come and find you there in the morning." With doubt in her eyes and her heart, Monica reluctantly agreed. She spent the night at the shrine praying for her children, and especially for Augustine, who had drifted so far from God. She prayed, with tears running down her face, that he had not deceived her, that he was not at that moment leaving Africa, that she would see him again in the morning. But morning arrived, and Augustine did not come for her. He was already far out to sea, making his way to Rome.

Keep on Running

Rome was awful. It did not help that as soon as he arrived, Augustine fell seriously ill. He spent most of the first month in bed. How he wished his mother was with him now. "Why did I treat her so terribly?" he asked himself. Augustine was afraid he might die, and wanted to know that she forgave him—but she did not even know he was ill!

He was staying with some Manichees, contacts of his Manichee friends in Carthage. They took good care of him all the time he was sick, but he no longer believed their talk of the light driving out his darkness, or at least not all of it, so their kindness made him feel bad, too, like an impostor.

It was not much better once Augustine recovered. He had dreamed of Rome as the city of Cicero and other great writers, where philosophy and learning would be valued, but if that city had ever existed, it was long gone. Now people were interested in dancing girls and chariot races, not seeking after the truth. Augustine was also painfully aware of how foreign he seemed. Only a few months before there had been a food shortage in Rome and many foreigners had been sent away from the city. Augustine stood out as one of a small number of non-Italians living in Rome. People made fun of his accent and his clothes, which were not at all fashionable by Roman standards. When people were rude to him about being an African, he just had to put up with it because often these were the same rich people whose help he needed, either to find students or to support him financially.

Money was difficult to start with, and Augustine had to be very careful with the funds that he had been given by rich supporters in Carthage. He used the money to set up a small school, teaching Latin and the art of public speaking. He knew that at the end of the academic year, when his students had to pay their fees, he would be much better off. It was true what they had told him in Carthage, that students were better behaved in Rome because they had the powerful City Prefect checking on them; there was no vandalism or rowdy parties. What Augustine had not been told, though, was that just before the end of the year, when fees were due, many students would switch to another school, leaving their teacher unpaid for all his months of work!

"I'm sick of it!" he complained to Alypius. "Every day I'm snubbed by people who care more about which flute player they should have at their banquet than about how they should live their lives. You're the only person I can talk to who understands."

"I know. Rome isn't what I expected either," said his friend. "So many arrogant people, treating you like a slave just because you're not rich and you weren't born in Italy."

"And showing off their wealth all the time! I can't count the number of times I've been shoved to the side of the road because some important person has to have twenty slaves with him wherever he goes, and I've even been to banquets where they weigh the food in front of you to impress you!"

Alypius laughed. He had been in Rome longer than Augustine, but he still found its ways strange, even after Carthage. Little Thagaste seemed like another world.

"Look, Augustine," Alypius suggested, "you're not happy here, so why stay? I've heard that the government in Milan is looking for a Professor of Rhetoric. Why don't you apply? You know that Symmachus has just become City Prefect, don't you, so he'll get to choose who's appointed. It's the perfect time!"

Milan, so far north, almost at the edge of the Empire! It was further than Augustine had ever dreamed of travelling—but it was also where the Emperor's court was. Nowhere could offer him a better opportunity to advance his career. Augustine grasped Alypius by the shoulders, smiling.

"I'm going to apply!"

Symmachus, Prefect of Rome, had lived in Carthage as governor of Africa while Augustine was teaching there. He knew of Augustine, and what was more, he knew he was a Manichee. Symmachus was a pagan, worshiping the old gods of his fathers. He hated the way Christianity was taking over the Empire. Milan, where his own cousin Ambrose was the bishop, was one of the places where it was strongest. Augustine might not have been a pagan, but at least he was not a Christian! Milan could do without any more Christians, Symmachus believed.

Symmachus had heard a lot about how good Augustine's public speaking was, but when the day came to demonstrate his talents, he turned out to be even better than the rumors. The Prefect listened to his speech with growing pleasure. This young African was excellent! When Augustine had finished speaking, and the applause had died down, Symmachus turned to his attendant.

"Make arrangements for travel to Milan for this young man and his family. He is the new Professor of Rhetoric."

* * *

Milan was at the center of government, and the edge of the world. In the city, people bustled round on important imperial business, dressed in fine clothes, papers in their hands. Meanwhile, beyond the mountains, not far away, Augustine knew there were hostile tribes of barbarians and even a false Roman emperor, ruling lands the real Western Emperor Valentinian II had no control over. In this smaller city, holding a government position, Augustine found himself quite an important person, not the nobody he had been in Rome. Being sent by Symmachus meant that the houses of all the Prefect's friends were open to Augustine. He had enough money, plenty of respectful pupils, and powerful supporters. He even had some of his closest friends with him, as Alypius had decided to move up from Rome, too, and Nebridius had come all the way from Africa to join them. He had Una, his girlfriend, living in his comfortable new home, along with their son Adeodatus, who was now twelve years old and showing a lot of promise in his education, taking after his father. But somehow, with all of these advantages, Augustine was not much happier in Milan than he had been in Rome. He had finally broken his links with the Manichees, since he no longer believed that they knew the truth, but now he saw no hope that he would ever find the truth. Perhaps there was no truth —or if there was, it could never be found. Augustine knew that many respected philosophers thought the same way, but it seemed rather depressing.

Augustine did have one very unexpected new interest to take his mind of things, however: he had started going to church! Symmachus would have been horrified, but Augustine did not think there was anything to worry about since what drew him to church was not silly stories about people long ago, but the preaching of Bishop Ambrose. Ambrose had been introduced to Augustine, of course, since he was Symmachus' cousin, but Augustine had already heard of him. He was a famous public speaker, even if he did only talk about the Bible.

So Augustine started attending church to hear the sermons, staying at the back with the other non-Christians. As a professional public speaker himself, it was great fun to watch Ambrose at work, and compare techniques with other speakers he had heard. He tried to ignore the content of the sermons and just appreciate the language, but Ambrose was too good a preacher not to get his message across.

As the weeks went on Augustine heard him explain passage after passage from the Bible. Many of them were from the Old Testament, the same stories that Augustine had found so off-putting when he was a teenager, but Ambrose found beautiful meanings in them that Augustine had never seen. Instead of seeing only bizarre tales of men with lots of wives and countless children living a backward life in the desert, Ambrose drew out messages of God's eternal faithfulness to his people, and signs of the Savior, Jesus, who was to be born centuries later. Eventually Augustine had to admit to his friends that he had misjudged the Christian faith. It was not absurd, as he had believed when he was a Manichee. In fact, it gave a reasonable explanation for most things—much better than Manicheanism.

What he had learned did not answer all of his questions, and Augustine was still bothered by the problem of how there could be evil in the world if

God was so good and powerful. However, he decided to put Christianity down as a potential source of truth – if truth existed at all. He had also heard rumors of a crackdown on Manichees starting in various places, since it was, after all, an illegal sect. It would be a good time to draw a line under that part of his life. Besides, Milan was a very Christian city and it would be an advantage to his career to have some sort of connection to the church. A few months after Augustine moved to Milan, when his mother came to join him, she was thrilled beyond words to discover that her darling son had become a catechumen—the first step to becoming a baptized Christian.

Monica had not lost her sense of ambition for her talented son, and seeing him in an important government position in Milan encouraged her to think about how far he could go.

"Just think, Augustine, here you are in the seat of government! In a few months you will give a speech of praise to the Emperor himself! This is your opportunity to make a great career for yourself. In a few years you could be set up for life, and your name could be known throughout the world—if you'll take my advice."

"What do you have in mind, Mother?" Augustine asked. "I'm already visiting all the important men in the city and my speeches are admired by everyone."

"Marriage," said Monica, bluntly. Augustine groaned. He knew his mother was right; what he really needed for a shining career was serious money, the money that only a rich wife could bring. A good marriage would also give him connections to high society in Milan. But what about Una?

"Mother, I love Una. She's given me a son. She's been good to me. I can't just send her away!"

Monica shook her head.

"That is something you should have thought of when you got tangled up in this relationship. You knew that eventually you would want to marry for your career, didn't you?"

Augustine nodded. It was never meant to have been permanent with Una, but year had followed year and they were still together.

"The decision is yours, Augustine," said Monica, "but I know of a well-placed Christian family here in Milan who would be willing to marry their daughter to you. But not if you have a girlfriend."

It was a difficult decision, but in the end there was only one choice for an ambitious man. With tears and apologies, Augustine broke off his relationship with Una. Adeodatus stayed with his father, but Una returned to Africa.

"I'll never have another man," she told Augustine, before she went. "There was only you, and there will only ever be you."

Augustine felt as if his heart was being torn to pieces. Soon, Monica arranged an engagement ceremony for Augustine and the young heiress he was to marry. She was sweet, pretty—and not much older than his son. Augustine put a brave face on it, smiling and charming his new in-laws, but inwardly he cursed his ambition, that had made him get rid of a good and loyal woman, just because she was not rich or important.

Sometimes Augustine just wanted to give it all up and go away somewhere with his friends to think about philosophy. Maybe that way he could eventually find the truth he was looking for. But it never seemed to be the right time, or his friends had wives and fiancées they couldn't leave. Instead he concentrated on his career, trying to fit in philosophy when he could—which was not very often, now that he was so busy.

If Augustine's work life was too busy thanks to his ambition, his private life was a mess due to his lack of self-control. It would be two years before his fiancée was old enough to marry him, and in the meantime he found another girlfriend, keeping her a secret from his mother. She took his mind off Una and his problems for a while, but when he thought about Una's promise to remain single Augustine felt ashamed and confused that he had not been able to control himself even for a few months.

To top it all off, there was the speech in praise of the Emperor to give. This was a great honor and a chance to advance his career, but everyone knew that when giving a speech of praise you were supposed to tell a pack of lies to flatter the person you were speaking about. The idea made Augustine uncomfortable, and the importance of the occasion curdled his guts with nervousness. He was walking through the streets with his friends, trying to take his mind off things, when they heard happy laughter. Ahead of them on the street was a beggar. He had obviously been drinking. He was laughing to himself and telling jokes. His merry smile brought home to Augustine just how unhappy he was.

"Look at this man!" he exclaimed. "He's happy, isn't he? We work hard and visit important men and tell lies and make ourselves sick with worry, in the hope that we will be successful, and then we'll be happy. But he is already happy, sitting here on the ground, with nothing!"

"But Augustine," said Alypius, "this man is drunk! Don't compare yourself to him!"

"He is drunk on wine, I am drunk on ambition. He at least will be sober tomorrow, but I won't! He got his wine by wishing passers-by well. I get mine by telling lies and twisting words. Am I so much better than him? Even if I ever get the success I want, will I really be happy? How is it possible that a drunk beggar is better off than us? What has gone wrong?"

Augustine's friends looked at one another but they had no answer. If there was a cure for Augustine's frustration and unhappiness, and for their own, they didn't know what it was.

Making the Leap

The elderly priest Simplicianus listened carefully to the young man pouring his heart out. It was obvious from his agitation that he was in a painful situation. He had started seeking the truth at a young age, he said, but had looked in the wrong places. Then he had let his ambition to be rich and important distract him from searching for truth, which was how he had come to Milan, but now he found that it did not satisfy him. He was in a job he no longer enjoyed, engaged to a girl he did not care about, feeling totally lost.

"So I turned back to philosophy," said Augustine, continuing the story of his life, "and starting reading some books by followers of the great philosopher Plato. To tell you the truth, they have been very helpful. I understand much better now that evil is not a substance with particles, fighting against good particles, as the Manichees say. It is something that's within our hearts. And I understand that God is not a substance, either, who fills the world like water in a sponge. Instead, he is spirit, a different sort of being altogether."

Simplicianus nodded. "I know these books you are talking about, and you are right that they contain a lot of truth, although not the whole truth. That is found only in the Bible. But tell me, were you reading these in Greek, or translated into Latin?"

"It was a Latin translation," Augustine said, "by a man called Victorinus. I believe he was a Christian."

Simplicianus smiled broadly.

"I thought so!" he said. "Victorinus was a great friend of mine, back when we lived in Rome. Let me tell you a story about him.

"Victorinus was Professor of Rhetoric in Rome, just as you are in Milan. He was highly educated and successful—so successful that they even put up a statue of him in the forum! But he was not a Christian when I first knew him. He worshiped the pagan gods, and not just the Roman ones but also the Egyptian ones, like the dog-headed god Anubis! He was enthusiastic about these cults, and spoke in public in their defence. But then one day he decided to examine the Bible and other Christian books. After a while he came to me privately and told me that he had become a Christian.

"'That's excellent!' I told him, 'But why do I never see you in church?' Victorinus tried to laugh this off, tried to say that it's not church walls that make someone a Christian, but he knew I was right. It would be embarrassing to admit to such a huge change of mind, and his friends would be very angry, so he hesitated, but by refusing to come out publicly as a Christian, he was denying Christ through his silence. Anyway, eventually he got up the courage to apply for baptism. Baptism candidates have to stand up in church and admit that they believe in Jesus. Victorinus was offered the chance to do this privately instead, since he was such an important man, but he refused.

"'I have spoken in public to defend the worship of false gods. Should I now be afraid to speak publicly about the one true God?' When he took to the stage to confess his beliefs, there was absolute silence. The church was crowded, but everyone wanted to hear if it was true. When Victorinus proclaimed that Jesus was God, his Savior, the crowd could not contain its enthusiasm! You should have heard the noise! It was a wonderful time."

Augustine nodded and tried to smile, but inside he was troubled. He understood why Simplicianus had told him this story—he saw a similarity with Augustine and hoped that it would encourage him to give his life to Jesus Christ, too. But somehow, he could not quite do it. Something held him back. He said a polite goodbye to the old priest and left.

Some time later, Augustine and Alypius received an unexpected visit in the home they shared with Nebridius and Monica. It was Ponticianus, another African who was working for the Government in Milan. Alypius went away to find the papers that Ponticianus had come to ask for, and the older man wandered around the room looking at things to pass the time.

"What's this?" he said, picking up a book that had been lying on a small table surrounded by dice and bits and pieces for gambling. "Some book of rhetoric, no doubt! You work too hard, Augustine, it is damaging your health." The government official looked more closely at the book.

"What? These are St Paul's writings! What on earth are you doing with these? Are you a Christian?"

"No, I'm not," admitted Augustine, "but I am very interested in Christianity. I have been attending Ambrose's sermons and reading the Bible."

"This is powerful material," chuckled Ponticianus. "Perhaps if you are not careful God's word will take you unawares and capture your heart, as it did to Anthony of Egypt!" By this time Alypius had returned to the room, and caught the end of the conversation.

"Anthony of Egypt? Who is he, sir?" he asked.

"Why, don't you know?" Ponticianus looked from one young man to the other, but they both shook their heads. "Then I must tell you about him!" he continued.

"Please do!" said Alypius, ushering the older man to a seat. When they had all made themselves comfortable, Ponticianus began his story. He told them of how Anthony, a young man from Egypt, was suddenly converted to Christianity one day when he heard the Bible being read out, and the words seemed to have been written just for him: "Go, sell all you have, give to the poor, and you shall have treasure in heaven. Then come, follow me." So he did! Then he went to live in the desert and devoted the rest of his life to prayer.

"It's a powerful story," said Alypius, when Ponticianus had finished.

"More powerful than you know! I have not done it justice at all. In fact, it changed the lives of two friends of mine. When we were wandering around near Trier one day, for we had some free time, these two stopped to spend an hour in the cottage of some Christians. There was a copy of the book *The Life of St Anthony*, and my friend began to read it. As I say, reading is dangerous work! His heart was set on fire and he immediately decided to give up his job as a government agent and devote his life to God. He explained his decision to my other friend, who was there with him in the cottage, and when he understood that he could become God's friend in an instant, well, he gave his life to the Lord too! They left their jobs, went away to live lives of Bible study and prayer, and they never looked back!"

Alypius laughed brightly at the inspiring story, but it was all Augustine could do to raise a weak smile. He felt like his soul was having a civil war. He *knew* that Jesus was the Truth he had been looking for, but he was holding back from giving his life to him. As soon as Ponticianus had left he turned to Alypius, and almost shouted,

"What's wrong with us? Anthony couldn't even read, but he could recognise the truth. Ponticianus' friends weren't highly educated, but they became friends of God. Here we are with all of our culture and education, rolling around in the mud of sin and ignorance! We should be ashamed of ourselves!" He was breathing fast, almost wheezing, his face was red and beads of sweat showed on his forehead. Alypius didn't know what to say, but before he could think of anything, Augustine headed for the garden, still with the book by St Paul in his hand. Alypius followed close behind him, saying nothing but unable to leave his best friend in this condition.

Augustine's face might have been flushed, and his movements frantic as he pushed his hands through his hair and rubbed his forehead, but that was nothing compared to what was going on inside him. Half of him—more than half of him—wanted to surrender to God, to accept the truth—for he knew now that Jesus was the Truth. But still he resisted, still he could not give up his old life. He thought of relationships with girls, of gambling and drinking games, of the attractions of power and prestige. Could he really give that up? Could he make this leap into the unknown? Ashamed of himself and his own weakness, he felt the tears welling up and moved further away from Alypius so that he could cry in privacy.

He was sitting under a tree, sobbing heavily, when suddenly his crying was interrupted by a child saying, "Pick up and read, pick up and read." Augustine looked up but he could see no one. Perhaps it was a child in a nearby garden playing a game. The voice came again:

"Pick up and read, pick up and read." Suddenly, Augustine wondered if this was a message. He remembered the story of Anthony and how his life had been changed by a verse from the Bible. Brushing the tears from his eyes he picked up the book by St Paul, opened it and read the first sentence he saw: "No orgies or drunkenness, no immorality or indecency, no fighting or jealousy. But put on the Lord Jesus Christ, and stop paying attention to your sinful nature and satisfying its desires." That was all it took. With a feeling of absolute relief, Augustine gave his heart to Jesus Christ.

Alypius was astonished to see Augustine walking back towards him, book in hand, looking more peaceful than he had in months. There were tear tracks on his face, but he was smiling.

"Alypius, I have finally done it—I have become a Christian. With God's help I am going to put my old life behind me and become a new man!" He told Alypius about the voice, and about reading the verses in the book. He would have expected Alypius to be happy, or at least playful, but he seemed very serious.

"May I see the passage?" he asked. Augustine handed him the book. Alypius pointed to the very next verse: "Welcome those who are weak in faith."

"That applies to me, Augustine." Alypius said. "I haven't searched for the truth as hard as you have, and I don't have your strength of belief, but I do believe that Jesus is the Savior, the only way to God. Welcome me, because I will now be a Christian too!"

Augustine hugged his friend, who was now also his brother. Then suddenly he remembered:

"My mother is in her room in the house! She has been praying for me to become a Christian for years and years. I must go and tell her immediately!" Alypius and Augustine rushed into the house to find Monica, almost knocking over a servant. In a great rush, with Alypius putting in some parts, Augustine told her what had happened.

"I hope you can forgive me for my arrogance, Mother."

"Praise God!" said Monica. "Augustine, I forgive you as God forgives you—completely! Praise God!" Augustine was delighted to see his mother so happy, with tears of joy rolling down her face, but he thought he had better be honest with her about what his decision meant.

"I will give up my career ambitions now, Mother. I want to devote myself to learning about God. And we will have to call off the marriage you arranged to help my career. I will probably never marry." Monica nodded, as if all of these things had already occurred to her.

"Don't you mind, Mother?" Augustine pressed her. "I won't be rich or famous, and I won't give you any more grandchildren." Monica laughed.

"What is money and fame in comparison with treasure in heaven? And what are future grandchildren in comparison with my dear son, who was dead and is alive again? I have no regrets, Augustine, and neither should you. Praise God!"

A New Life

Augustine was on fire again, but this time it was not with lust or ambition. Instead, he was burning with passion for God and with gratitude at being freed from his old life. He had already decided that he would give up his job at the end of the academic year, and he could hardly wait as the last few weeks of the summer term crawled past. He had been thinking of giving up work in public speaking anyway, at least for a while, because his weak chest had started to trouble him, but now he could look forward to a completely new stage in his life—a life he had decided to dedicate to God.

As soon as the autumn holidays began, Augustine and some of his friends and family left Milan to stay in a country villa that their rich friend Verecundus had kindly lent them. The villa was at Cassiciacum, a peaceful spot surrounded by mountains and lakes, with shady hideaways for hot days and its own bathhouse for when the wintry weather set in, as it did early in the mountains. Augustine felt pure, sweet relief to be away from all the complications of Milan and to have the time to explore his new faith. He knew that he should learn more about Christianity before he applied for baptism, so he threw himself into prayer and Bible reading. The Psalms came alive for him, now that he had the Spirit of God to help him, and he felt as if Psalm 4, by King David, had been written especially for him. Tears fell from his eyes as he read the words: "I was in terrible distress, but you set me free. Now have pity and listen as I pray."

Although he loved to spend time alone with God, Augustine had not lost his enjoyment of spending time with other people, and especially of talking about philosophy. Here, away from the world, he was surrounded by many of the people he loved most—his mother, brother and son, along with Romanianus' son Licentius and a few of Augustine's other former pupils. Every day they had philosophical discussions about the nature of the soul, or education, or how people can be certain about the truth. As Augustine's body recovered from the stress of Milan, he devoted himself to leading his little group of philosophers.

He had been so preoccupied with work that it was a surprise to him, as well as a delight, to discover how well his teenaged son Adeodatus already understood the Christian faith, which his mother Una had taught him about. It was also a great joy for Augustine to be able to learn from his own mother. For so long he had assumed that he was much cleverer than her, that she did not really understand how things were. Now he saw that his mother had the deep wisdom that comes from a life lived with God, something his expensive education could not compare to. Monica felt as if she had got her son back, and Augustine felt that he was coming to know his mother fully for the first time.

It was with some sadness that, after many wonderful months at Cassiciacum, Augustine told his friends that he would have to leave.

"The winter is really coming on, and I must go back to the city before we get snowed in. I need to be in Milan to put my name forward for baptism this coming Easter, and to be prepared for baptism by Bishop Ambrose. The process will take the rest of the winter."

"In that case, I must return with you," replied Alypius, "for I will ask Ambrose for baptism, too! There's no going back now, not for me."

"Nor for me," chipped in Adeodatus. "I may be young, but I know what I believe. Let's all be baptized this Easter—if you give your permission, Father." Augustine embraced his son.

"I shouldn't have expected any less of you! You are a fine son, and soon you will also be my brother in baptism! We should start making preparations to leave at once."

* * *

On the evening of Easter Saturday in the year AD 387, Augustine, Alypius and Adeodatus, along with all the other candidates for baptism, entered the silent baptistery in Milan. Bishop Ambrose, whom Augustine had come to know well during his baptism preparations, carried out the solemn act. Afterwards, dressed in white robes and with cold water still dripping from their hair, the three friends entered the main church to stand before the congregation as newly baptized Christians. The church blazed with candles, throwing reflections off the marble pillars and gold decorations. The air was perfumed with incense, and the echo of singing filled every corner of the building. Grateful for Christ's salvation, sure of the truth, and overflowing with the emotion of the occasion, Augustine let the tears of joy run down his cheeks.

Afterwards, Augustine and his Christian friends talked about what direction their lives should take.

"We are all agreed," said Augustine, "that we want to form a community where we can live quiet lives devoted to Christian studies. The question is, where should we go? We cannot occupy Verecundus' villa forever, and there is nothing to hold any of us here in Milan, is there?" Evodius spoke up. He was a man from Thagaste that Augustine and his friends had come to know since their return to Milan for baptism. He had turned his back on his job in the secret police to become a Christian.

"We are all Africans, aren't we?" asked Evodius. "Not only that, we are all from the same town. You come from Thagaste, Augustine, as does your mother. So do you, Alypius, and you, Severus. God has brought together this group of people from a small town in

Africa, who have all become Christians during their travels throughout the world. Now, perhaps, it is time to go back to where we started—to Thagaste?"

"It is striking, isn't it?" said Alypius. "Perhaps this is the route we are supposed to take—back to Africa."

"Well, let us pray about the issue, and if we are all agreed, we will make plans to go back to Africa straight away!" said Augustine.

Soon, the little group was making arrangements to return to their homeland. The plan was to travel by road to Rome, then take a ship from Ostia, Rome's nearest port, across to Carthage, where they could complete the rest of the journey overland. Unfortunately, things did not go as smoothly as planned. The famous commander Maximus, who had made himself emperor of Britain, Gaul and Spain, was no longer satisfied with only the north-western part of Europe; he wanted to be ruler of the whole Roman Empire. Augustine and his group were still on their way to Rome when the news reached them that Maximus had crossed the Alps, invaded Italy, and driven the emperor Valentinian II out of Milan! The young emperor had fled to Greece, and no one knew what Maximus' next move would be. That became clear when they finally reached Rome. Maximus was blockading the city! No ships could get in or out. They could go no further on their journey until the situation changed.

Augustine and his friends had no way of knowing how long the blockade would last, so they decided to stay at Ostia, the port, to be ready to leave as soon as Maximus and his ships sailed away. As friends of the great Bishop Ambrose, they were welcomed in by a rich Christian family who had plenty of room to spare. They settled down to wait out the rest of the summer.

For Augustine, it was a good time. He might not have made it back to Africa yet, but he was in a quiet town, surrounded by his friends and family, with plenty of time to get on with his studies and writings about God. He was working on a book explaining how the beliefs of the Manichees, which had seemed so convincing to him once, were actually full of mistakes and could not solve the problem of sin. As well as discussing issues like this with his group of friends, Augustine was glad to have time to spend alone with his mother. He had always loved her, but they had grown so close since he had become a Christian that they seemed to understand each other in a way no one else did.

"What do you think eternal life is like?" he asked her once, as he gazed out of the window, watching the sun flood the beautiful courtyard garden.

"Look at all this beauty in front of us, Augustine! The sunshine, the scent of the flowers! Heavenly life must be far, far above all of these earthly pleasures." They talked on and on, about knowing God perfectly in the life to come, about his perfect love and wisdom, until they almost felt as if they were approaching heaven themselves.

"We can have some idea of what heaven is like, Augustine," said Monica when they had reached the end of their discussion, "but the reality will be so much better. As for me, I am ready to go and be with God. All I wanted in life was to see you become a Christian —and here you are, devoting the rest of your life to God! There is nothing more I want in this life."

Augustine embraced her and smiled, unaware that his mother's desire would be granted much more quickly than he could guess. Five days later, Monica caught a fever and went to her bed. She never got out of it again. Two weeks after their conversation about heaven, Monica was dead.

Closing his mother's lifeless eyes, Augustine felt as if he would burst with grief, but he kept a tight hold on himself. He thought that if he showed his sadness it would be as if he thought something bad had happened to his mother, when in fact she had gone to be with God. Adeodatus cried as he stood at his grandmother's bedside, but the others comforted him and Evodius led them in songs of joy from the Bible to celebrate Monica's life and faith.

They arranged to bury Monica there in Ostia. People came to pay their respects before the funeral, and Augustine pushed down his grief and would not let himself cry. Even as they prayed by the grave side, he swallowed his tears, but he could not get rid of the pain. He prayed to God to take the pain away, and tried to take his mind off what had occurred, but nothing worked. That night, Augustine went to bed feeling heavy with grief, and fell asleep tired out from the pain he was trying to ignore. In the morning, though, it seemed that God had answered his prayer. It was not that Augustine did not feel sadness at his mother's death, but suddenly, alone in his room and remembering everything that made Monica so dear to him, he realized that he could weep for the person he had lost, and God would not misunderstand him. He poured his heart out in prayers and tears, and felt wonderful comfort and release.

By the time anyone was ready to make plans again after Monica's death, autumn was coming on and the safe season for sailing was almost at an end. There did not seem to be much point in waiting any longer at Ostia, so the group of Christians from Thagaste headed back to Rome until the following year. It was strange for Augustine to be back in the city he had disliked so much, but with his group of Christian friends, and without his burning ambition, it seemed a different place than before. He spent the long winter completing his book against the Manichees, and grieving for the wonderful companion, counsellor, friend and mother he had lost in Ostia.

A New Path

"It is good to be home!" declared Augustine, leaning back on a bench, with his face turned up into the warm African spring sunshine. "I think I will never leave Thagaste again!"

Alypius laughed.

"You're just saying that because you hate travelling, Augustine, not because you love Thagaste!" Augustine shielded his eyes to look at his friend.

"Well, that is probably true. But why would I need to leave again? I have all my closest friends here with me. We have our family estates to support us. We have the rest of our lives to learn about God. We no longer have duties or ambitions that require us to travel all over the Empire. Let us stay still, and be thankful!"

Alypius laughed again, but did not disagree. Augustine had every right to hate travelling, when his mother had died en route, and there were rival emperors at sea, stirring up wars. As for himself, he had not lost his taste for travel just yet, but why shouldn't Augustine enjoy the quiet life for a change?

Despite its quietness, Augustine's community of Christians soon became quite well-known in Africa. It was hardly surprising; high-flying lawyers and politicians had given up their careers to study God. This was not an everyday occurrence. Augustine found himself receiving written questions and visits from many important Africans, and becoming friends, through letters, with some of the best-known Christians in the Roman world.

Many times a visitor would raise the idea of Augustine becoming a priest or a bishop, but he could not imagine it. He wanted to get away from career and responsibilities so he could spend time with God. Bishops had no end of responsibilities, and spent a lot of time travelling, so they had less time to spend with God than the average person! Besides, he worried that priesthood, being too much like the career he had left, might tempt him back into the sins of excessive ambition and pride. In fact, Augustine was so keen to avoid this life that he would not even visit towns that were missing a bishop, since he knew he might be forced to take on the role. That was how Ambrose had become bishop of Milan, after all. Instead, if anyone from a town without a bishop wanted to consult Augustine, they had to come and visit him.

It had been almost fifteen years since Amatus' death, and Augustine's sadness had faded enough so that his hometown did not cause him pain any more, but it seemed that Thagaste had not finished inflicting tragedy on Augustine. First it was Nebridius. Although he had joined them in Milan, Augustine's old friend had not been able to join the community at Thagaste. His family had huge estates near Carthage, and he needed to keep an eye on them for at least part of the year. He and Augustine had kept in touch by letter, and had hoped to see more of each other in the future, but this hope was never fulfilled. Only a year after he had come back to Thagaste, Augustine saw a messenger with a sombre face approaching his villa. He knew the man, a resident of Carthage.

"What's the news from Carthage, my friend?" he asked, approaching him. "Is there a war? Or do you have news of Nebridius? I hope the illness he wrote to me about has not become more severe?"

The man shook his head sadly.

"I wish I had better news. Nebridius' illness did become much more severe. He is dead."

This was a hard blow for Augustine, especially as he had not visited his friend during his illness, and had missed his last chance to enjoy Nebridius' intelligent conversation and to learn from his wisdom. But worse was to come. Later that same year, Adeodatus came down with a fever. This was nothing unusual—many people became sick at the turn of the seasons, and Adeodatus was not the only one to take to his bed. Augustine had no fears for him, for he was young and strong, not approaching old age like Monica. Once again, though, Augustine's hopes proved false. His son's youth and strength could not stop the course of the fever. By the end of the year he, too, was dead. He was only eighteen.

Once again, Augustine found himself visited by death in Thagaste. This time, however, not only were those who had died baptized Christians, he was a Christian himself. Although Adeodatus had been very young, and Nebridius barely middle aged, he knew that they were with God, and that he would see them again. Instead of being bitter about the part of their lives that they would not get to live, he thanked God for the lives that they had lived, for the way they had been able to help and guide other people, and for the fact that they had been friends of his, and friends of God.

Even so, Augustine did spend a little more time outside Thagaste after the loss of his son. In fact the community was getting a bit too big for Augustine's family villa, because more people had heard about it and come to join it. Now when he went to other towns Augustine kept an eye open for a place that he and his friends could start a proper monastery. This was on his mind when he went to visit the large, ancient town of Hippo Regius. A friend in Hippo had written to tell Augustine that he was seriously thinking about Christianity, and wished to talk about it with him. Augustine could hardly refuse, so he made his way through the mountains up to the coast, wondering if this town might be a suitable place for his community of Christians. He was not worried about visiting, because he knew that Hippo already had a bishop, a Greek called Valerius.

Augustine spent a few days with his friend, and on the Sunday attended the service at Hippo's church. People had heard that he was staying in the town, and a few heads turned to watch him as he took his place in the center of the church. The educated men of the town had heard good things about his community in Thagaste, and many of them had also read Augustine's books, for he had found plenty of time to write about Christianity since he had given up his career in Milan. Augustine tried to ignore their gossiping as he settled himself to listen to the sermon.

Valerius was elderly, but he was passionate. He spoke, with a heavy Greek accent, about the problems facing Hippo, the villages in the region that were barely reached, the people preaching false religion or trying to undermine the church.

"I am getting older, my children, and the work is too much for me. I need another priest to help me here in Hippo. If anyone knows of a suitable person, bring him to me at once!" Immediately, Augustine felt a hand take hold of his arm, and another hand clap him on the shoulder.

"Here is Aurelius Augustine, of Thagaste!" shouted a voice.

"Augustine from Milan!" shouted another.

"Augustine, Augustine!" people began to chant. Against his will, Augustine felt himself moving towards the front of the church, where Valerius waited in his high bishop's chair. His sandals skidded on the stone floor as he tried to resist the hands gently, and not so gently, urging him forwards.

"No, please don't! This is not the life I've chosen! I just want to live quietly!" Augustine's protests were ignored.

"He's just being modest," he heard a voice say. "Give him another push."

As the bishop's chair grew nearer and nearer, Augustine saw his life of quiet study slipping away. Tears began to fall down his cheeks, but even this form of protest was misunderstood.

"He's upset because he's not being made bishop straight away. Don't worry, sir, you'll be a bishop in a few years, and being a priest is almost as good!"

Eventually Augustine was pushed right up to Bishop Valerius himself. The bishop extended his hand to Augustine.

"Aurelius Augustine, do you accept the holy position of priest in our church?" Augustine looked behind him at the expanse of keen faces, smiling, nodding and shouting. He knew he had no choice. This might not be the life he had chosen, but it seemed to be the one God had chosen for him. He nodded.

"Then I shall ordain you as priest of Hippo! Welcome to your new home!"

Valerius might have taken Augustine away from Thagaste, but he had no intention of taking his monastery away from him.

"Let them all come!" he said. "The church has very big gardens. Build your monastery there, live with your friends. Only, help me with the preaching. My Latin is not so good, and I struggle with it."

So Augustine found himself in the community he had hoped for after all, living with his friends and with others who had come to join them, surrounded by beautiful gardens, and able to study the Bible and write books as before. But he did not have as much spare time, because Valerius had been very serious about the preaching. Normally, only the bishop preached, but Valerius knew that his new priest was one of the best public speakers in Africa, and he intended to make good use of him. Right from the start, Augustine started speaking in the church, teaching the people about God. The churchgoers were amazed, and word spread. Soon, people were coming from nearby towns to hear Augustine, and others started writing his sermons down as he spoke so that they could send them to people who lived further away. They were so popular that local uneducated priests started getting hold of copies of them so they could read Augustine's sermons to their churches instead of struggling to write their own. But even that was not enough to satisfy Valerius.

"You were a Manichee, Augustine," he said one day. "People know this. Fortunatus, the Manichee priest, is a powerful speaker and is leading people away from the truth. Church members have asked if you will debate with him in public. What do you say?"

"I know Fortunatus. We were Manichees together in Carthage. If he is willing to have a debate, I would be happy to try and lead him to the truth."

The debate was set up in a public bathhouse, neutral ground for both of them. Fortunatus tried to hide his nervousness as he greeted his old friend. He was aware of Augustine's reputation, and he had heard him speak convincingly in favor of Manichaeism back in Carthage. Could he be just as convincing now he believed that those beliefs were wrong?

It turned out that he could. Over two days, Augustine answered all of Fortunatus' questions, and asked him many questions that he could not answer. At the end of the second day it was clear that Fortunatus had lost.

"I don't know the answers to your questions, Augustine. I shall consult Manichees who are higher up than I am. If they cannot answer these questions either —well, I will have to consider where the truth really lies." Fortunatus left the town shortly afterwards to seek the answers to his questions. He never returned to Hippo.

Meanwhile, whenever his duties allowed it, Augustine enjoyed the life of his little monastery, where everyone shared what they had with each other, and gossip was forbidden. Many of the men who had come to join the community were not from the same educated background as Alypius, Evodius and Augustine, and the former teacher enjoyed teaching these new students about how to understand the Bible and deepen their relationship with God. The community was so successful in producing men who really understood the Bible that, after a few years, nearby towns needing a priest or a bishop started asking members of Augustine's community to take up the roles. One of the first to go was Alypius. A few years after their move to Hippo Regius, he moved back to his hometown, this time as its bishop. Augustine was sad to see his friend leave, but he knew that he would be a wonderful bishop for the people of Thagaste — and, since Alypius had no problem with travelling, they would still see each other often. Meanwhile, the monastery stayed strong, for every time someone left to be a priest or bishop, others would come to take their place.

One of the members who had been there almost from the beginning, from soon after Augustine founded the Monastery in the Garden, was a young man called Possidius. He was of a simple, African background, but he greatly admired Augustine and wanted to devote his life to God in the same way. It was a new thing for Augustine to have close friends who were not university-educated, but he found that their down-to-earth attitude and their ability to understand the local people were valuable, and in fact he could learn from them as well as them learning from him. These new friends were also a source of support for Augustine when he felt disappointed that his new life had not turned out the way he had planned. On a day like this, seeing that Augustine was feeling discouraged, Possidius approached his new friend in his usual straightforward way:

"Augustine, I know you never chose to be priest of Hippo. I know you didn't plan to spend your time writing sermons and preaching in church. But I have seen how much good those sermons are doing. They are teaching the people—and inspiring them—here and in lots of other towns, too. I just wanted to say—I think God had chosen an excellent priest."

Trouble at Home,
Trouble Abroad

"It's my cow!"

"No it's not! Father wanted me to have it!"

Augustine rubbed his forehead and tried to concentrate. It was his seventh case this morning. He had not been wrong about bishops' duties taking up a lot of time. Since he had become bishop of Hippo Regius, after Valerius died in AD 396, every morning was taken up with sorting out arguments among the townsfolk—that is, when he wasn't travelling to other towns on official business. He listened carefully to these two brothers fighting over the inheritance that their father had left them, then gave the wisest judgement he could. The brothers walked away, muttering but willing to accept his decision. A crowd of people parted to let them through on their way out. The rest of the crowd were waiting for decisions from Augustine, too. Praying to God for wisdom, and trying not to sigh, Augustine called out,

"Next!"

It was not just in local matters that Augustine required wisdom. There were bigger problems throughout the whole of Africa, too, and one of the biggest ones was a breakaway church called the Donatists. The Donatists were Christians, like Augustine, but they did not want anything to do with the rest of the church. They believed that they were the only pure Christians, and all the others were stained by sin. Nearly a hundred years earlier, before the Roman emperors had become Christians, an emperor called Diocletian had stamped down hard on Christianity. He had tried to force people to give up their faith, and to prove it by handing over their Bibles. It was a terrifying time. Some people had resisted the Emperor's orders, and been killed or tortured. Others had handed over their Bibles, but secretly remained Christians, waiting for the persecution to end.

The persecution stopped after a few years, but a different kind of trouble started. Some people said that any priest who had handed over his Bible could never be a priest again. If a 'traitor' priest baptized someone, it did not count, and if he gave the bread and wine of communion, it was not really communion. To top it all off, if a 'traitor' priest made someone else a priest, that person wasn't really a priest at all. Since no one was completely sure who had handed over their Bibles and who had not, some people did not trust the church at all—it might be full of fake priests. So they set up their own church, instead, the Donatist church.

Augustine was used to winning people over by using reason, and he applied himself to the problem of the Donatists. He knew there were lots of Donatists in Hippo and the rest of Africa, especially in the countryside, so he wrote pamphlets, gave talks and offered to debate with Donatist leaders. These were all the things that worked well with the Manichees. The Donatists were different, though. They did not want to debate, and they did not want anything to do with the impure church Augustine belonged to.

"They must see reason," Augustine said to his friends. "God can forgive anyone, even people who denied him out of fear. After all, didn't St Peter do that —and he was welcomed back by Christ himself!" He shook his head. "If they were right, the only true church would be in Africa, and all the Christians in the whole of the world are not really Christians at all! They must be able to see that's not true." But the Donatists did not see it.

There was another thing that made Donatists different from Manichees: violence. Most Donatists were peaceful, but some of their supporters were anything but. These were large groups of travelling vagabonds called Circumcelliones—the Graveyard Gang—because they hung around the tombs of saints. They had no homes or jobs of their own, but wandered about vandalizing, attacking people, and causing trouble. They attacked landowners and officials, as well as anyone who disagreed with them, especially priests and bishops from the normal church.

It wasn't long before Augustine had a narrow escape from the Graveyard Gang himself. He was making a visit to a nearby town. The journey had not gone well, and Augustine disliked travelling at the best of times. He was tired and fed up, and just wanted to rest, but the bishop he was visiting ran out of his house and dashed up to Augustine as if there were some emergency.

"You've arrived, thank God!" cried the local bishop. "I didn't have any way to warn you. How did you escape?"

"What are you talking about?" asked Augustine irritably. "We got lost and took the wrong road, that's why we're so late. What do you mean, how did we escape?"

"Augustine, you don't know how lucky you have been today," replied the bishop. "I got word that the Graveyard Gang were waiting to attack you. They had heard you were coming and they staked out the road— the right road. Thank God you came by the wrong road! That mistake may have saved your life."

Not all of Augustine's friends were so lucky. Possidius, who had joined the Monastery in the Garden in Hippo, was now bishop of Calama. Like Augustine, he tried to open talks with the local Donatist bishop, who was called Crispinus, but Crispinus did not want to know. Soon after Augustine's lucky escape, some of Crispinus' followers caught Possidius while he was travelling near Calama. They attacked him with wooden clubs and drove him off the road. Possidius ran into a nearby house and barred the door. He had just stopped panting and had started to check how bad his wounds were, when he smelled smoke. Fire! The Donatist supporters had set fire to the house. Trapped between the fire and a group of thugs with weapons, Possidius did not know what to do. Eventually, when he could hardly breathe from the smoke, he pushed open the door. Crispinus' thugs were gone – but so were his donkeys and all of his luggage.

Possidius talked to Augustine and they agreed that something had to be done; the time had come to use the law. Bishop Crispinus had done nothing about the attack, he had not even criticized his followers, so Possidius took Crispinus to court. Crispinus was found guilty of heresy and ordered to pay ten pounds of gold, but Possidius spoke to the court officers so that the fine would not be collected.

"It's the principle," he explained to the court officers. "Crispinus should now realize that he's wrong, so there's no need to actually take the money from him." But Crispinus did not realize that he was wrong. In fact, he was so angry at being found guilty that he appealed to the Western Emperor himself.

The Emperor Regent, Stilicho, was not impressed. Donatists did not even consider anyone outside of their sect to be a true Christian – and that included him! They ignored the authorities and thought they were above the law. What was more, they had already been involved in two revolts in Africa! There had been Firmus back in the 70s, and only a few years ago the Donatist Count Gildo has risen up against the Western Emperor, and

Stilicho had had to send an army against him. Now the Donatists wanted him to protect them against the normal church? Some chance! Stilicho wrote back that Crispinus should pay the fine, and the court officers should pay a fine, too, for letting him get away without paying the first time. Once again, Possidius made sure that no one actually had to pay—after all, surely now the Donatists had lost the argument?

But Donatist violence continued. The Graveyard Gangs especially hated people who stopped being Donatists and joined the main church. The bishop of a town called Bagai had done just this. Not long after the attack on Possidius, the Graveyard Gang of Bagai assaulted the bishop, but this time they went further. They chased him into his church. He hid under the altar to try and escape, but they smashed it with their clubs while he was still underneath it. Then they kept on smashing once they had broken through, until they were sure the bishop was dead. That night, they threw his body on to a rubbish heap outside the town. But the Bishop of Bagai was not dead. In the morning, a citizen passing the rubbish heap heard him groaning weakly, found the injured man, and rushed to get help.

When he had recovered enough to travel, the furious Bishop of Bagai set out for Ravenna in Italy, to the court of the Western Emperor, to ask for harsh measures against the Donatists. He spoke passionately, but the scars from his attack were more effective than any speech. Emperor Honorius and Emperor Regent

Stilicho were convinced. They made Donatism illegal. Donatist priests and bishops were stripped of their status, and Donatist churches were closed down. Anyone who disobeyed could have their property confiscated—or even be executed!

Now Augustine found himself with a lot of work to do. He had to welcome many ex-Donatists into his church, making sure they received proper teaching, and that the other Christians did not discriminate against them. He gave sermons and debates, and put up posters showing that the Donatists were wrong, because there were plenty who stuck to their "pure" church even once it was illegal. He recruited priests who spoke Punic, the local language, to go into the countryside to teach African villagers the truth. On top of all this, he tried to persuade the officials who had the job of punishing Donatists, not to use the death penalty.

"We love our enemies, and we pray for them," he wrote to the Proconsul in charge of Africa. "We didn't appeal to judges and laws because we want the Donatists dead, but because we want them to be saved from their mistakes, and from the danger of God's eternal judgment. Please remember my request, and forget all about your legal right to execute them!"

The Donatist situation took up so much of Augustine's time and attention that it almost seemed to be the biggest problem in the world. He was so concerned with his affairs in Africa that he did not pay much attention to the rest of the Roman Empire, except when his colleagues went to Italy to see the Emperor about the Donatists. That was about to change. There had been news and rumors for years about bands of barbarians moving around in Roman territory, and new rival emperors taking power in the northwest, just as Maximus had years before. Twice in the past few years, armies of Goths had got into Italy, even as far as Rome, but both times the Barbarians had retreated. Now, in summer AD 410, Augustine could no longer ignore the crisis across the sea. Refugees started to arrive in Africa with only a few belongings, and with unbelievable news: Rome, the heart of the Empire, had been taken by the Goths.

The Last Push

Africa was in uproar. True and false reports, rumors, out-of-date and up-to-date news, and refugees—thousands of refugees—flooded in from Italy. There was talk of the total destruction of Rome, while others said the damage was not so bad. Many reported that the Goths had already left Rome, and some added that they were on their way to Africa! Augustine did his best to calm tensions and to help the refugees settle in, while he waited for the full picture to emerge. Eventually it became clear that, while the destruction had been shocking, and many people had died, the attack on Rome had actually only lasted three days before the Goths left the city and moved south. It had looked as if they were trying to reach Africa, but their ships were destroyed by a storm, and now they were heading north again. The Christians who told Augustine this had seen the events with their own eyes, and they reported that the Goths had not attacked the churches:

"We sheltered in the churches, hundreds, thousands of us! We were terrified. But Alaric, the leader of the

Goths, told them not to attack us. Anyone who stayed in a house of God was safe. It was a miracle!"

Not everyone was so willing to see God's hand in the events across the sea. It was not only Christian refugees who had come to Africa seeking a new life after their city had been ransacked. There were also pagans, worshipers of the old gods. They saw the attack on their city in a completely different light. Augustine heard their grumblings during his visits to Carthage, which he had to make often during that troubled time.

"This is what comes of forgetting the old gods!" muttered one old man outside a wine shop.

"You're right!" replied his companion, more loudly. "The gods will not be ignored. What did we sacrifice for, all those years, if not to get the good will of the gods? Centuries of honoring the gods, making sacrifices, putting on festivals—and Rome conquers the whole world! Then the emperors convert to Christianity—goodbye sacrifices, festivals, respect for the gods, and goodbye Rome!" He thumped his tumbler down on the table and red wine splashed out like blood, as if to prove his point.

Augustine knew that it was not only in Carthage that people were saying and thinking these things. He was tired and overworked and he was getting ill, but still, he knew something had to be done to combat these views. He kept the issue in mind as he spent some time towards the end of the year in a country retreat, recovering his health. The following year he attended a final, great conference to decide the Donatist question once and for all, along with his friends Possidius, Alypius and Evodius, all of whom were now bishops. As he had done many times before, Augustine used his amazing powers of public speaking to show, patiently, rationally and finally, that the Donatists were in the wrong. The imperial commissioner Marcellinus, who was to judge the debate, came down on the side of the mainstream church. The argument had finally been won.

But there was no time for Augustine to rest now. The questions of the pagans had not gone away. Marcellinus, who was a friend of Augustine, had many hard questions for Augustine about how Christianity fitted in with running a state. He wanted Augustine's help to answer the pagans who were criticizing the Roman Empire's decision to turn to Christianity. A pagan political leader, Volusian, also wrote to Augustine asking him deep questions about Christianity, to see if it could stand up to his philosophical debates with his friends. At first Augustine tried to cover all these issues in letters that he sent, which Marcellinus could share with his friends, but the questions kept coming. Finally, Augustine realized that God was leading him towards something much bigger than a few letters.

"I feel that the time has come to write a book—a great big book," he told his fellow residents of the monastery as they sat around the long wooden table, eating their simple food. "In it I will answer the mistaken beliefs of those people who say that Rome fell because we neglected the false gods, but I will do much more than that. I will try, with God's help, to give an outline of the whole story—creation, judgement, eternity, angels and demons, everything! And I will show how all people have to be citizens either of God's kingdom, or of the devil's. Please pray that God would help me in this great work!"

A short time later, Augustine sat down and began the first part of his enormous new project. He was in his fifties now, and he knew that this might be his last big work of philosophy, his chance to share the truth with as many people as possible.

"Here, my dear Marcellinus," he wrote, "is the fulfilment of my promise, a book in which I have taken upon myself the task of defending the glorious City of God against those who prefer their own gods."

This great book alone would have been enough to keep Augustine busy, but he did not get the free time he would have liked to concentrate on it. It was not only pagan ideas that had come to Africa with the refugees. New Christian ideas had, too, and some of them were very worrying. Marcellinus told him that in Carthage now there were followers of the British monk Pelagius. People held conflicting opinions about Pelagius. Some said that he wanted to encourage self-control and good morals in Christians, to make them understand that to carry on sinning after being baptized was rebellion against God. That sounded excellent. Others reported that he made out that Jesus was just a good example, not the Savior, and that people could save themselves by their own efforts. Some friends sent Augustine a book by this Pelagius so that he could make his mind up for himself.

Augustine was impressed. Pelagius was clearly an intelligent and thoughtful man. His book was full of serious philosophical arguments and it did indeed encourage Christians to live good, self-controlled lives. Unfortunately, there was a big problem. Pelagius thought that people had the ability to stop sinning and be good by their own efforts. He thought that if they only tried hard enough they could be perfect. There was no need to rely on God's grace, no need to pray for his help, as Jesus had instructed his disciples to do. Instead, Pelagius seemed to be suggesting that people could save themselves from sin. That would mean that Jesus' death on the cross had been for nothing.

Augustine was becoming an old man, and after his battles with the Manichees and Donatists he did not need another war of words, but he realized that he had to write a reply to Pelagius' book. There was a real danger that people who had not been forgiven by God, by accepting Jesus' sacrifice, would be persuaded by Pelagius that there was no need. They might think all they needed was a strong effort to be good. Augustine, looking back on his life, knew that this was just an illusion. It was hard enough not to sin even after he had received the Holy Spirit, although he prayed every day for help. Without God's help, it was utterly impossible. He thought about his youthful self, struggling against sexual urges and ambition for riches and fame. No amount of effort had helped; it was divine grace that had set him free. With weariness, but a sense of great responsibility, he once again took up his pen to write to Christians about their need for the one who "helps them when they try, and hears them when they pray."

Of course, just one letter did not persuade Pelagius and his supporters that they were wrong. Many more letters followed, back and forth, and debates were held on the subject. The Pope and the Western Emperor were convinced that Augustine was right about the need for God's help, and they condemned the Pelagians, but still the argument stretched on and Augustine spent more and more of his strength on this, his final philosophical battle.

Outside the world of philosophy, though, there were plenty of other things using up the old man's strength. When Rome had been taken by the Goths, some people had thought that the end of Rome signalled the end of the world. Rome was in fact still standing, but it had started to look as if maybe the world *was* coming to an end—at least the Roman world that Augustine and his friends knew. There were Goths in Italy, Vandals in Spain, and Huns just beyond Roman borders. No one could remember a time when Rome had been in so much danger from barbarians, not since the foundation of the city. Places on the edge of the Empire, like Britain and Armenia, were falling out of Roman control and there seemed to be no way to stop it.

It was not just real barbarians that were dangerous, either. There were unscrupulous Romans who would dress as barbarians to swoop down on the African coast in fast boats and kidnap women and children to sell them as slaves. One group of pirates collected all of their prisoners together in Hippo Regius itself, while they got ready to transport them to slave markets overseas. Augustine was away on one of the many journeys that he had to make as bishop, but fortunately the congregation of his church found out what was happening. Horrified, they clubbed together to buy the poor frightened people out of slavery before they could be transported across the world.

Despite all of this turmoil, and his ongoing debates with the Pelagians, Augustine somehow managed to finish the huge book he had started. "With God's help I have completed this great work," he wrote in AD 426, as he finished book twenty-two, the final part of *City of God*. It had taken him thirteen years and he was now a very old man, in failing health—but the book was a masterpiece.

Now that this enormous book was out of the way, Augustine took some time to look back over his other works. He put together a list of all the books and sermons he had written, and as he went through them he added bits, deleted bits, or made corrections where there were mistakes. He realized that he might not have much longer and he wanted to make his body of work as good as it could possibly be so that it might help others to find the truth—the truth by which he had lived his life.

It was not only Augustine who did not have much time, though. His homeland was under threat, too. The barbarians who had taken over Spain were on the move again. In AD 429 the Vandals crossed the sea to Africa.

The End

Possidius pushed through the crowds as he made his way towards the Monastery in the Garden. He had never seen Hippo this crowded, not even during the biggest festivals. A group of goats, scared by the noise and crowds, rushed past him, brushing roughly against his legs and nearly knocking him over. Their owner dashed after them carrying his staff, shouting, "Woah there, come back!" Huddling in a doorway, two children buried their heads in an older woman's skirt. He could not hear their sobs above the noise of the street, but Possidius could see their shoulders jerking as they cried. The woman, perhaps their grandmother, did not look far from tears herself.

Most of these people were here for the same reason that he was. They were escaping from the Vandals. The tales about the Goths in Rome, which everyone had found so shocking at the time, were nothing compared with what was happening in Africa. The Vandals, unlike the Goths, did not respect churches or ministers of God. In fact, they tortured priests, thinking they must be rich, and burned many churches to the ground. Stories of their cruelty had spread through the land faster than the smoke from the towns and villages they had burned. Those who could, left their homes and escaped to somewhere safer, to the big cities with walls and defences, to Cirta, Carthage, and Hippo Regius. Some had managed to pack their belongings and even bring their farm animals. Others had only managed to take a few things that they could carry on their backs. Many had escaped with nothing at all, running desperately through fields and vineyards while the barbarians burned their village and killed their neighbors. Calama, where Possidius was bishop, was one of the towns that had fallen to the Vandals, so here he was, along with everyone else, trying to find safety behind the high walls of Hippo.

At least he knew he would find a warm welcome back at the monastery. Augustine helped anyone who was in need, and they were old friends.

"Welcome, Possidius!" the elderly bishop cried. Possidius was sad to see how much more frail Augustine looked than the last time they had met, but it was clear that he was unchanged in other ways. He still had that twinkle in his eye, the warmth and wit that people were often surprised to find in such a deep thinker. "I'm sorry for what brings you to Hippo," he went on, "but I can't say I'm sorry to have you here. Come on, have some dinner with me and tell me all the news." They went to the common dining room, where everything was as it had been when Possidius was a young man here, down to the wooden plates and the little poem on the table forbidding gossip.

Possidius had plenty of news to tell, although no doubt it was the same thing that Augustine had been hearing from everyone else: The Vandals were marching east across Africa. Count Boniface, the commander of the Roman army, was trying to stop them, but so far he was failing. Calama had fallen, and it looked as if the Vandals would soon reach Hippo.

"Well, I pray that God will protect us, and the people of our church," said Augustine when he had listened to all Possidius had to say, "but I also pray that God will give us the strength to endure whatever happens. After all, as Bishop Ambrose said before his death, 'I do not fear to die, for we have a Lord who is good.' And now, let's talk about something more cheerful!"

Possidius was not the only bishop who had to flee when the Vandals took over towns. Many other bishops and priests escaped from their towns and villages along with the members of their church, and some ran away alone as soon as they heard that the Vandals were coming. Some did not escape in time, and were killed, while others deliberately stayed behind until the Vandals arrived, because they did not want to run away while any of their church members were still in danger. There was a lot of disagreement about what was the right thing to do, because no one had ever lived through a time of such great danger before. Once again, Augustine's wisdom was in demand.

A bishop called Honoratus wrote to him asking what was the right thing for bishops and priests to do. Should they stay and serve the people of their church, or should they run away and save themselves so that they would survive to serve the church again in the future? After all, St Paul himself had escaped from Damascus when his life was in danger, and didn't the Bible say that when you were treated badly in one city you should flee to another? What was the point of staying just to watch people being killed?

Augustine could understand the temptation of Honoratus to persuade himself that running away was the right thing, but he knew it was not really.

"St Paul escaped when his enemies were only looking for him, not for everyone," he wrote back to Honoratus. "As long as there are Christians in your town who need you, that's where you should be. If everyone else has run away, of course you can escape too, but if there are still Christians there, they need a priest. After all, it is often when they are in danger of death that people realize that they need God. It is more important that their souls are saved than their bodies." Augustine sent the letter off with a trusted messenger, and prayed that Honaratus and all the priests and bishops he passed it on to would be able to be brave, and stay with the people who needed them.

Not long after this, prayers became the only kind of messages that Augustine was able to send, because no one could get in or out of Hippo. Count Boniface and his army had been pushed further and further back by the Vandals. Now he, too, had come into Hippo Regius, and was trying to continue the war from behind the walls. Outside, Vandals surrounded the city on all sides. Even the sea was closed to the Romans; the Vandals blocked the port with their ships.

Everyday life continued inside the besieged city. Weeks turned into months. The Vandals could not get in, and Count Boniface could not drive them away. The city was even more crowded now the troops were here, and huge crowds swept into Augustine's church to hear him preach. As he had predicted, now that life seemed less certain and death looked much closer, people were desperate to know about eternal life, and the one who had defeated death. As long as his strength held out Augustine gave his world-famous sermons to the packed church, but he could not go on forever. He was now seventy-six. Augustine had often been ill, sometimes seriously, but now that he was an old man he did not have the strength to fight off diseases. In August of AD 430, Augustine came down with a bad fever, and he realized it would be his last.

"How is Bishop Augustine," Possidius asked the doctor who was coming out of Augustine's room. The doctor shrugged.

"He gets weaker and weaker. He might last a few more days, or even a week or two, but no longer." Possidius made to go into the bedroom to see his friend but the doctor gently stopped him, with a hand on his sleeve.

"He does not want to see anyone. He has asked me to tell everyone only to visit him at mealtimes, or when I am examining him. He wants to spend the rest of the time he has left preparing himself to meet God."

Inside the room, tears rolled down Augustine's face as he thought about all the sins he had committed, not just before his baptism but even after he became a Christian. He wondered if he had behaved well in all the religious arguments that had made up his life as a bishop. Had he always acted out of love? He knew that, although he had always taught people the truth as he honestly understood it, there had been times when his teaching had been harsh, or arrogant. He read the psalms of David, which had been posted up on his wall at his request: "The Lord has heard my weeping. The Lord has heard my cry for mercy. The Lord accepts my prayer." Augustine's tears continued to fall as he thought about all the times he had disobeyed God, but there was no fear in his heart. He knew that he was forgiven.

A few days before the month of August was out, Augustine died. His funeral was simple, as he would have wanted, and he had no will because he did not have any important possessions to leave to anybody. What he had left, though, was his magnificent library. Feeling sad but peaceful after the funeral, Possidius walked around Augustine's library, the room where he had written so many useful letters, so many great works. His pen still lay on the desk where he had left it. Augustine had given up a career that could have made him very rich, but in its place he had built this treasure trove of words, an entire life's work dedicated to helping people find and understand the truth that had meant everything to him.

"Augustine," said Possidius to the empty room, his throat tight with tears, "was like the merchant in Jesus' parable who went looking for fine pearls. When he found the most wonderful pearl, he sold all he had to get it. But it was worth it. It was worth it."

Augustine Timeline

AD

354   Augustine is born at Thagaste on
       November 13th.

365   Goes to school in Madaura.

370   Returns to Thagaste from Madaura.

371   Goes to Carthage for the first time to
       study rhetoric.

372   Finds a girlfriend. His father dies.

373   Falls into the Manichean error.
       His son Adeodatus is born out of wedlock.

375   Returns from Carthage to Thagaste to
       teach rhetoric.

376   Death of friend who was baptized.
       Returns to Carthage and begins
       teaching rhetoric.

380   Writes *De Pulchro et Apto* (lost work).

383   Sails to Rome with girlfriend and son.

384   Appointed Professor of Rhetoric in Milan.

386   Augustine converted in a garden in
       Milan. Retreats with his mother, Adeodatus
       and his friends to Cassiciacum, to devote
       himself to Christianity.

387   Returns to Milan, he and his son are baptized.
       His mother dies.

390   Returns to Carthage, then Thagaste;
       his son dies.

391	Ordained a priest in Hippo, North Africa.
392	Writes to St Jerome requesting Latin translations of Bible commentaries. Debates in Hippo with Fortunatus, the Manichee.
393	Assists the plenary Council of Africa and delivers a discourse which later became one of his works: *On Faith and the Creed*.
396	At age 42 becomes Bishop of Hippo.
397	Writes work against the Epistle of Mani, called the *Fundamental*.
401	Completes the story of his own conversion, his Confessions. Writes work against Faustus, the Manichee.
403	The Donatist controversy.
411	Attends a conference at Carthage on June 11 to debate against the Donatist and successfully overthrows their doctrine.
412	Pelagianism condemned at a council held at Carthage for their attacks against the doctrine of Original Sin.
420	Completes his work on the Trinity.
421	Writes the *Enchridion of Faith, Hope and Love*.
426	Completes his monumental work: *The City of God*.
427	Writes his Retractions.
430	Augustine dies at Hippo on August 28th at 76 years old.

Thinking Further Topics

Chapter One – A Brush With Death
No one knows exactly how long they will live. Imagine you knew you were going to die tomorrow. How would that change your behavior, and your attitude to people and to God? What about if it was in one week, or in one hundred years?

Chapter Two – Bad Company
Augustine followed his friends' bad example at school and at home in Thagaste. How can you resist peer pressure? Do you think you are a good influence or a bad influence on your friends?

Chapter Three – Love, but No Marriage
Augustine thought that his mother's advice about sex before marriage only applied to girls. If you were Monica, what would you have said to him?

Chapter Four – Looking for Wisdom
What do you think of the lessons Augustine found in the book by Cicero? How can you judge whether ideas and philosophies are good or bad? Who could you talk to for advice on this?

Chapter Five – Divided Loyalties
Monica prayed for years and years that her son would

become a Christian. Is there anything that you have been praying for for a long time? How can you avoid getting discouraged?

Chapter Six – Running Away
How could Augustine have handled the situation better when Monica did not want him to leave? Do you ever tell lies to make life easier? Is it ever okay to lie?

Chapter Seven – Keep on Running
Do you think Augustine was right when he compared himself with the drunk beggar? Augustine later said: "you have made us for yourself, and our hearts are restless until they rest in you." True happiness is found in God. Where else were Augustine and his friends trying to find it? Where do you try to find it?

Chapter Eight – Making the Leap
Why did Victorinus think it was so important to declare his beliefs publically? Do you find the stories of other Christians inspiring? If you are a Christian, do you ever share the story of how you came to believe?

Chapter Nine – A New Life
Do you ever think about the 'big questions', as Augustine and his friends did? About heaven and hell, what God is like, and how you should live your life? Who can you talk to about these things? Where could you find out more information?

Chapter Ten – A New Path

Augustine's skills were used by God in a completely different way from what he expected. What plans do you have for your life? How flexible would you be if God had a different plan for you? Where does what God wants rank in your list of priorities?

Chapter Eleven – Trouble at Home, Trouble Abroad

The Donatists were not prepared to forgive people who had betrayed their faith. What do you find hard to forgive? God says we should forgive others the same way He forgives us (Matthew 6:12). What have you done that needs to be forgiven?

Chapter Twelve – The Last Push

Pelagius thought that people could stop sinning without God's help. Augustine disagreed. Do you think you can be totally good through your own efforts? Do you think anybody can?

Chapter Thirteen – The End

The priests and bishops who were afraid of the Vandals were unsure about the right thing to do. What would you have advised them to do? Where could you go for advice if you were ever in a dangerous situation?

Notes on Names

Augustine never gave the name of his long-term girlfriend in any of his writings. The biographer Garry Wills called her Una because Augustine said that he had only lived with one woman (*una* is 'one' in Latin), and I have borrowed this idea from him.

Augustine also never gave the name of the close friend in Thagaste who died. I have used the name Amatus, which means 'beloved' in Latin, because Augustine loved him so much.

Augustine did get up to no good with a group of boys in Thagaste during his year off from school. He did not record any of their names. I have given the ringleader the name Iatanbaal because that was a common pagan name in North Africa at the time. It means 'given by Baal'.

Father Crispus, the priest in Thagaste, and the slaves Paula and Marcus also have invented names. All the other names in the book are real.

Quotes and Paraphrases from Augustine's Writings

Chapter Eleven
Request not to use the death penalty. Letter 100.

Chapter Twelve
The first line of Augustine's great book. *City of God* I.i
(Penguin 1972, translated by Henry Bettenson)
God "helps them when they try, and hears them when
they pray." *On Nature and Grace* 81

Main Sources

St Augustine, *Confessions* (translated by Henry
Chadwick), Oxford University Press, 1991.

Possidius, *The Life of St Augustine* (translated by Herbert
T. Weiskotten), Arx, 2008.

Peter Brown, *Augustine of Hippo*, University of
California Press, 1967.

Susan Raven, *Rome in Africa*, Routledge, 1993.

Gillian Clark, *Late Antiquity*, Oxford University Press,
2011.

Quotes and Paraphrases from the Bible

Chapter Three
"There is a time for everything, and a season for every activity under the heavens." (Ecclesiastes 3:1)

Chapter Four
"God made human beings that resembled him." (Genesis 1:27)
"Put to death your earthly desires." (Colossians 3:5)
"Set your minds on things above." (Colossians 3:2)

Chapter Eight
"No orgies or drunkenness, no immorality or indecency, no fighting or jealousy. But put on the Lord Jesus Christ, and stop paying attention to your sinful nature and satisfying its desires." (Romans 13:13-14)
"Welcome those who are weak in faith." (Romans 14:1)

Chapter Thirteen
"The Lord has heard my weeping. The Lord has heard my cry for mercy. The Lord accepts my prayer." (Psalm 6:8-9)
The merchant who bought the fine pearl.
(Matthew 13:45-46)

CHRISTIAN FOCUS PUBLICATIONS

Christian Focus | Christian Heritage | CF4K | Mentor

Christian Focus Publications publishes books for adults and children under its four main imprints: Christian Focus, CF4K, Mentor and Christian Heritage. Our books reflect our conviction that God's Word is reliable and Jesus is the way to know him, and live for ever with him.

Our children's publication list includes a Sunday School curriculum that covers pre-school to early teens, and puzzle and activity books. We also publish personal and family devotional titles, biographies and inspirational stories that children will love.

If you are looking for quality Bible teaching for children then we have an excellent range of Bible stories and age-specific theological books.

From pre-school board books to teenage apologetics, we have it covered!

Find us at our web page:
www.christianfocus.com

CF4·K
Because you're never
too young to know Jesus